You shall be as gods

Other Books by Erich Fromm

ERICH FROMM

You shall be as gods

A RADICAL INTERPRETATION

OF THE OLD TESTAMENT

AND ITS TRADITION

Holt, Rinehart and Winston

NEW YORK   CHICAGO   SAN FRANCISCO

Unless otherwise noted, the Scripture quotations in this publication are from the *Revised Standard Version of the Bible*, copyrighted 1946 and 1952 by the Division of Christian Education, National Council of Churches, and used by permission.

All Talmudic translations are from the Soncino Talmud, published by the Soncino Press, London, 1948, under the editorship of Rabbi Dr. I. Epstein, with an Introduction by the editor.

Designer: Ernst Reichl
8611600
Printed in the United States of America

Foreword

I want to express my gratitude to all those who have generously helped me in the completion of this book. Mr. Neal Kozodoy has read the whole manuscript and has made important critical and constructive suggestions that have considerably improved the book. Professor James Luther Adams, Professor Kristar Stendhal, Monsignor Ivan Illich, Father Jean Lefèvbre have been most generous in helping my understanding of the Christological literature in connection with the story of the Passion. Mr. Arthur A. Cohen has also contributed valuable criticism and suggestions, and Mr. Joseph E. Cunneen has greatly helped the manuscript with his thoughtful and constructive editing.

I want to thank most warmly Miss Beatrice Mayer, who for fifteen years has not only typed and retyped all my manuscripts with great care, including this one, but who has also done a first and very helpful editing of the text.

E. F.

Contents

You shall be as gods

i *Introduction*

Is the Hebrew Bible, the Old Testament, more than a historical relic to which polite reverence is paid because it is the fountainhead of the three great Western religions? Has it anything to say to man today—man living in a world of revolutions, automation, nuclear weapons, with a materialistic philosophy that implicitly or explicitly denies religious values?

It would hardly seem that the Hebrew Bible could still be relevant. The Old Testament (including the Apocrypha) is a collection of writings by many authors, written during more than a millennium (about 1200 to 100 B.C.). It contains codes of law, historical accounts, poems, prophetic speeches,

3

only a part of a larger literature produced by the Hebrews during these eleven hundred years. * These books were written in a small country on the crossroads between Africa and Asia, for men living in a society that neither culturally nor socially had any resemblance to ours.

We know, of course, that the Hebrew Bible was one of the main inspirations not only of Judaism but also of Christianity and Islam, and thus deeply influenced the cultural development of Europe, America, and the Near East. Yet it seems today that, even among Jews and Christians, the Hebrew Bible is not much more than a respected voice of the past. Among most Christians the Old Testament is little read in comparison with the New Testament. Furthermore, much of what is read is often distorted by prejudice. Frequently the Old Testament is believed to express exclusively the principles of justice and revenge, in contrast to the New Testament, which represents those of love and mercy; even the sentence, "Love your neighbor as yourself," is thought by many to derive from the New, not the Old Testament. Or the Old Testament is believed to have been written exclusively in a spirit of narrow nationalism and to contain nothing of supranational universalism so characteristic of the New Testament. Indeed, there is encouraging evidence of changes in attitudes and practice both among Protestants and Catholics, but much remains to be done.

Jews who attend religious services are more familiar with the Old Testament, since a portion of the Pentateuch is read each Sabbath, and on Mondays and Thursdays as well, and

* For a short and concise literary history of the Old Testament, I recommend Robert H. Pfeiffer, *The Books of the Old Testament,* 2nd ed. (New York: Harper & Row, 1948).

the entire Pentateuch is completed once every year.* This knowledge is further increased by the study of the Talmud, with its innumerable quotations from the Scriptures. While those who follow this tradition are a minority of Jews today, this way of life was common to all until only about a century and a half ago. In the traditional life of the Jews the study of the Bible was fostered by the need to base all new ideas and religious teachings on the authority of biblical verses; this use of the Bible, however, had an ambiguous effect. Because biblical verses were employed to support a new idea or religious law, they were often quoted out of context, and an interpretation was imposed on them which did not correspond to their real meaning. Even where no such distortion occurred, there was often more interest in the "usefulness" of one verse in support of a new idea than in the meaning of the total context in which it occurred. In fact, the text of the Bible was better known via the Talmud and the weekly recitations than through direct, systematic study. The study of the oral tradition (Mishnah, Gemara, and so on) was of greater importance and a more exciting intellectual challenge.

Throughout the centuries the Bible was understood by the Jews not only in the spirit of their own tradition but also, to a considerable extent, under the influence of the ideas of other cultures with which their scholars had contact. Thus Philo saw the Old Testament in the spirit of Plato; Maimonides in the spirit of Aristotle; Hermann Cohen in the spirit of Kant. The classic commentaries, however, were written in

* The reading of the Pentateuch is followed by a chapter from the Prophetic writings, thus blending the spirit of the Pentateuch with that of the Prophets.

the Middle Ages; the most outstanding commentator is R. Solomon ben Isaac (1040–1105), known as *Rashi,* who interpreted the Bible in the conservative spirit of medieval feudalism.* This is true even though his and other commentaries on the Hebrew Bible clarified the text linguistically and logically, and often enriched it by turning to the haggadic compilations of the rabbis, the Jewish mystic lore, and sometimes to Arabic and Jewish philosophers.

For the many generations of Jews after the end of the Middle Ages, especially for those living in Germany, Poland, Russia, and Austria, the medieval spirit of these classic commentaries helped to reinforce the tendencies rooted in their own ghetto situation, where they had little contact with the social and cultural life of the modern age. On the other hand, those Jews who, beginning with the end of the eighteenth century, became part of the contemporary European culture had, in general, little interest in studying the Old Testament.

The Old Testament is a book of many colors, written, edited, and re-edited by many writers in the course of a millennium and containing in itself a remarkable evolution from primitive authoritarianism and clannishness to the idea

* Rashi's explanation of the first sentence in the Bible is a good example: "The reason for commencing with the creation is to justify the allocation of the Holy Land to Israel; for God being the Creator of the World, He can assign any part of it to whomsoever He desires." The narrowness of Rashi's comment is striking. Where the text speaks of the creation of the world, Rashi thinks of the Jewish claim to Israel and, along the lines of feudal custom, proves that God, being the owner of the entire world, has the right to give a piece of land to whomever he pleases. (This, and all other translations of commentaries to the Bible throughout this book, are quoted from the Soncino *Chumash,* edited by A. Cohen [Hindhead, Surrey: The Soncino Press, 1947].)

of the radical freedom of man and the brotherhood of all men. The Old Testament is a *revolutionary* book; its theme is the liberation of man from the incestuous ties to blood and soil, from the submission to idols, from slavery, from powerful masters, to freedom for the individual, for the nation, and for all of mankind.* Perhaps we, today, can understand the Hebrew Bible better than any age before, precisely because we live in a time of revolution in which man, in spite of many errors that lead him into new forms of dependence, is shaking himself free of all forms of social bondage once sanctioned by "God" and the "social laws." Perhaps, paradoxically enough, one of the oldest books of Western culture can be understood best by those who are least fettered by tradition and most aware of the radical nature of the process of liberation going on at the present time.

A few words must be said about my approach to the Bible in this book. I do not look at it as the "word of God," not only because historical examination shows that it is a book written by men—different kinds of men, living in different times—but also because I am not a theist. Yet, to me, it is an extraordinary book, expressing many norms and principles that have maintained their validity throughout thousands of years. It is a book which has proclaimed a vision for men that is still valid and awaiting realization. It was not written by one man, nor dictated by God; it expresses the genius of a people struggling for life and freedom throughout many generations.

While I consider the historical and literary criticism of

* It is the revolutionary character of the Old Testament which made it a guide for the revolutionary Christian sects before and after the Reformation.

the Old Testament highly significant within its own frame
of reference, I do not believe that it is essential to the purpose of this book, which is to help in the understanding of
the biblical text, and not to give a historical analysis; however, where it seems important to me to refer to the results
of historical or literary analysis of the Hebrew Bible I will
do so.

The editors of the Bible did not always smooth out the
contradictions between the various sources they used. But
they must have been men of great insight and wisdom to
transform the many parts into a unit reflecting an evolutionary process whose contradictions are aspects of a whole.
Their editorship, and even the work of the sages who made
the final choice of the Holy Scriptures, is, in a broad sense,
a work of authorship.

The Hebrew Bible, in my opinion, can be treated as *one*
book, in spite of the fact that it was compiled from many
sources. It has become *one* book, not only through the work
of the different editors but also through the fact that it has
been read and understood as one book for the last two thousand years. In addition, individual passages change their
meaning when they are transferred from their original
sources into the new context of the Old Testament as a
whole. Two examples may serve as an illustration for this.
In Genesis 1:26 God says: "Let us make man in our image."
This, according to many Old Testament scholars, is an
archaic sentence introduced by the editor of the Priestly
Code without much change. According to some authors the
sentence conceives of God as a human being. This may be
perfectly true as far as the original archaic meaning of the
text is concerned. But the question arises why the editor of
this passage, who undoubtedly did not have such an archaic

concept of God, did not change the sentence. I believe the reason is that for him the sentence meant that man, being created in God's image, has a Godlike quality. Another example is the prohibition to make an image of God, or to use his name. It may very well be that originally this prohibition derived its meaning from an archaic custom found in some Semitic cults of considering God and his name as taboo; hence, they forbade making his image and using his name. But in the context of the entire book the meaning of the archaic taboo has been transformed into a new idea: namely, that God is not a thing, and therefore he cannot be presented in a name or in an image.

The Old Testament is the document depicting the evolution of a small, primitive nation, whose spiritual leaders insisted on the existence of one God and on the nonexistence of idols, to a religion with faith in a nameless God, in the final unification of all men, in the complete freedom of each individual.

Jewish history did not stop when the twenty-four books of the Old Testament had been codified. It went on and continued in its fuller course the evolution of ideas that had begun in the Hebrew Bible. There were two lines of continuation: one is expressed in the New Testament, the Christian Bible; the other in the Jewish development that is usually called the "oral tradition." The Jewish sages have always emphasized the continuity and unity of the written tradition (the Old Testament) and the oral tradition. The latter was also codified: its older part, the Mishnah, around A.D. 200; its later part, the Gemara, around A.D. 500. It is a paradoxical fact that precisely from the standpoint which takes the Bible for what it historically is, a selection of writings over many centuries, it is easy to agree with the traditional view regarding the unity between the written and the oral traditions. The oral tradition, like the written Bible, contains the record of ideas expressed over a span of more than twelve hundred years. If we could imagine that a second Jewish Bible were to be written, it would contain the Talmud, the writings of Maimonides, the kabbalah, as well as the sayings of the Hasidic masters. If we could visualize such a collection of writings, it would cover only a few centuries more than the Old Testament, it would be composed by many authors living under entirely different circumstances, and it would present as many contradictory ideas and teachings as the Bible does. Of course such a second Bible does not exist and for many reasons could not have been compiled. But what I want to show by this idea is that the Old Testament represents the development of ideas over a long period of time, and that these ideas have continued developing during an even longer period, after the Old Testament had been codified. This continuity is dramatically and visually demonstrated on any given page of a Talmud printed today: it contains not only the Mishnah and Gemara but also subsequent commentaries and treatises written down to the present day, from before Maimonides to after the Vilna Gaon.

The Old Testament and the oral tradition both contain contradictions within themselves, but the contradictions are of a somewhat different character. Those in the Old Testament are largely due to the evolution of the Hebrews from a small nomadic tribe to a people who lived in Babylonia and were later influenced by Hellenistic culture. In the period following the completion of the Old Testament, the contradictions lie not in the evolution from archaic to civilized life; they lie more in the constant split between various opposing trends going through the whole history of Judaism from the destruction of the Temple to the destruction of the centers of traditional Jewish culture by Hitler. This split is that between nationalism and universalism, conservatism and radicalism, fanaticism and tolerance. The strengths of the two respective wings—and many sectors in between— have, of course, their reasons; they are to be found in the specific conditions of the countries in which Judaism developed (Palestine, Babylonia, Islamic North Africa and Spain, Christian medieval Europe, Czarist Russia) and in the specific social classes where the scholars originated. *

The foregoing remarks point to the difficulty in interpreting the Bible and the later Jewish tradition. Interpretation of an evolutionary process means showing the development of certain tendencies that have unfolded in the process of evolution. This interpretation makes it necessary to select those elements that constitute *the* main stream, or at least *one* main stream in the evolutionary process; this means weighing certain facts, selecting some as being more and others less representative. A history that ascribes the same

* The distinction between the "right wing" and the "left wing" is most clearly expressed in two of the earliest representatives among the Pharisees: Hillel and Shammai. When a heathen came to Shammai and asked him to explain the whole Torah while standing on one leg, Shammai threw him out. When he came with the same request to Hillel, he received the following answer: "The essence of the Torah is the command: Do not do unto others as you should not want them to do unto you—the rest is commentary. Go and study." In a brilliant book, *The Pharisees* (Philadelphia: The Jewish Publication Society of America, 1962), Louis Finkelstein has shown the differences between the right and the left wing among the Pharisees and has analyzed their social background. For a profound study of two such "schools of thought" in medieval Jewry, see Jacob Katz, *Exclusiveness and Tolerance* (Oxford: Oxford University Press, 1961).

importance to all facts is nothing but an enumeration of events; it fails to make sense of the events. Writing history always means interpreting history. The question is whether the interpreter has sufficient knowledge of, and respect for, the facts to avoid the danger of picking out some data to support a preconceived thesis. The only condition which the interpretation in the following pages must fulfill is that the passages from the Bible, the Talmud, and the later Jewish literature should not be rare and exceptional utterances but statements made by representative figures and part of a consistent and growing pattern of thought. Furthermore, contradictory statements must not be ignored, but taken for what they are: part of a whole in which contradictory patterns of thought existed side by side with the one emphasized in this book. It would require a work of much greater scope to offer proof that radical humanist thought is the one which marks the main stages of the evolution of the Jewish tradition, while the conservative-nationalistic pattern is the relatively unchanged relic of older times and never participated in the progressive evolution of Jewish thought in its contribution to universal human values.

Although I am not a specialist in the field of biblical scholarship, this book is the fruit of many years of reflection, as I have been studying the Old Testament and the Talmud since I was a child. Nevertheless, I would not have dared to publish these comments on Scripture were it not for the fact that I received my fundamental orientation concerning the Hebrew Bible and the later Jewish tradition from teachers who were great rabbinical scholars. All of them were representatives of the humanistic wing of the Jewish tradition, and strictly observing Jews. They differed greatly, however, from each other. One, Ludwig Krause, was a traditionalist, little touched by modern thought. Another, Nehemia Nobel, was a mystic, deeply steeped in Jewish mysticism as well as in the thought of Western humanism. The third, Salman B. Rabinkow, rooted in the Hasidic tradition, was a Socialist and a modern scholar. Although none of them left any extensive writings, they were well known to be among the most eminent Talmudic scholars living in Germany before the Nazi holocaust. Not being a practicing or a "believing" Jew, I am, of course, in a very different position from theirs, and least of all would I dare to make them responsible for the views expressed in this book. Yet my views have grown out of their teaching, and it is my conviction that at no point has the continuity between their teaching and my own views been interrupted. I was also encouraged to write this book by the example of the great Kantian Hermann Cohen, who, in his *Die Religion der Vernunft aus den Quellen des Judentums*, used the method of looking at the Old Testament together with the later Jewish tradition as a whole. Even though this little work cannot compare with his great opus, and although my conclusions sometimes differ from his, my method has been strongly influenced by his way of looking at the Bible.

The interpretation of the Bible given in this book is that of radical humanism. By radical humanism I refer to a global philosophy which emphasizes the oneness of the human race, the capacity of man to develop his own powers and to arrive at inner harmony and at the establishment of a peaceful world. Radical humanism considers the goal of man to be that of complete independence, and this implies penetrating through fictions and illusions to a full awareness of reality. It implies, furthermore, a skeptical attitude toward the use of force, precisely because during the history of man it has been, and still is, force—creating fear—which has made man ready to take fiction for reality, illusions for truth. It was force which made man incapable of independence and hence warped his reason and his emotions.

If it is possible to discover the seeds of radical humanism in the older sources of the Bible, it is only because we know the radical humanism of Amos, of Socrates, of the Renaissance humanists, of the Enlightenment, of Kant, Herder, Lessing, Goethe, Marx, Schweitzer. The seed becomes clearly recognizable only if one knows the flower; the earlier phase is often to be interpreted by the later phase, even though, genetically, the earlier phase precedes the later.

There is one more aspect of the radical humanist interpretation that needs to be mentioned. Ideas, especially if they are the ideas not only of a single individual but have become integrated into the historical process, have their roots in the real life of society. Hence, if one assumes that the idea of radical humanism is a major trend in the biblical and post-biblical tradition, one must assume that basic conditions existed throughout the history of the Jews which would have given rise to the existence and growth of the humanistic tendency. Are there such fundamental conditions? I believe there are and that it is not difficult to discover them. The Jews were in possession of effective and impressive secular power for only a short time, in fact, for only a few generations. After the reigns of David and Solomon, the pressure from the great powers in the north and south grew to such dimensions that Judah and Israel lived under the ever increasing threat of being conquered. And, indeed, conquered they were, never to recover. Even when the Jews later had formal political independence, they were a small and powerless satellite, subject to big powers. When the Romans finally put an end to the state after R. Yohanan ben Zakkai went over to the Roman side, asking only for permission to open an academy in Jabne to train future generations of rabbinical scholars, a Judaism without kings and priests emerged that had already been developing for centuries behind a façade to which the Romans gave only the final blow. Those prophets who had denounced the idolatrous admiration for secular power were vindicated by the course of history. Thus the prophetic teachings, and not Solomon's splendor, became the dominant, lasting influence on Jewish thought. From then on the Jews, as a nation, never again regained power. On the contrary, throughout most of their history they suffered from those who were able to use force. No doubt their position also could, and did, give rise to national resentment, clannishness, arrogance; and this is the basis for the other trend within Jewish history mentioned above.

But is it not natural that the story of the liberation from slavery in Egypt, the speeches of the great humanist prophets, should have found an echo in the hearts of men who had experienced force only as its suffering objects, never as its executors? Is it surprising that the prophetic vision of a united, peaceful mankind, of justice for the poor and helpless, found fertile soil among the Jews and was never forgotten? Is it surprising that when the walls of the ghettos fell, Jews in disproportionately large numbers were among those who proclaimed the ideals of internationalism, peace, and justice? What from a mundane standpoint was the tragedy of the Jews—the loss of their country and their state —from the humanist standpoint was their greatest blessing: being among the suffering and despised, they were able to develop and uphold a tradition of humanism.

ii *The Concept of*
GOD

Words and concepts referring to phenomena related to psychic or mental experience develop and grow—or deteriorate—with the person to whose experience they refer. They change as he changes; they have a life as he has a life.

If a six-year-old boy says to his mother, "I love you," he uses the word "love" to denote the experience he has at the age of six. When the child has matured and developed into a man, the same words spoken to a woman he loves will have a different meaning, expressing the wider range, the greater depth, the larger freedom and activity that distinguish the love of a man from that of a child. Yet while the experience to which the word "love" refers is different in the child and in the man, it has a common core, just as the man is different from the child and yet the same.

There is simultaneously permanence and change in any living being; hence, there is permanence and change in any concept reflecting the experience of a living man. However, that concepts have their own lives, and that they grow, can be understood only if the concepts are not separated from the experience to which they give expression. If the concept becomes alienated—that is, separated from the experience to which it refers—it loses its reality and is transformed into an artifact of man's mind. The fiction is thereby created that anyone who uses the *concept* is referring to the substratum of *experience* underlying it. Once this happens—and this process of the alienation of concepts is the rule rather than the exception—the idea expressing an experience has been transformed into an *ideology* that usurps the place of the underlying reality within the living human being. History then becomes a history of ideologies rather than the history of concrete, real men who are the producers of their ideas.

The foregoing considerations are important if one wants to understand the concept of God.

They are also important in order to understand the position from which these pages are written. I believe that the concept of God was a historically conditioned expression of an inner experience. I can understand what the Bible or genuinely religious persons mean when they talk about God, but I do not share their thought concept; I believe that the concept "God" was conditioned by the presence of a socio-political structure in which tribal chiefs or kings have supreme power. The supreme value is conceptualized as analogous to the supreme power in society.

"God" is one of many different poetic expressions of the

highest value in humanism, not a reality in itself. It is unavoidable, however, that in talking about the thought of a monotheistic system I use the word "God" often, and it would be awkward to add my own qualification each time. Hence, I wish to make my position clear at the outset. If I could define my position approximately, I would call it that of a nontheistic mysticism.

To which reality of human experience does the concept of God refer? Is the God of Abraham the same as the God of Moses, of Isaiah, of Maimonides, of Master Eckhart, of Spinoza? And if he is not the same, is there nevertheless some experiential substratum common to the concept as used by these various men, or might it be that while such a common ground exists in the case of some, it does not exist with regard to others?

That an idea, the conceptual expression of a human experience, is so prone to be transformed into an ideology has its reasons not only in man's fear of committing himself fully to the experience, but also in the very nature of the relationship between experience and idea (conceptualization). A concept can never adequately express the experience it refers to. It *points* to it, but it *is* not it. It is, as the Zen Buddhists say, "the finger that points to the moon"—it is not the moon. One person may refer to his experience by the concept *a*, or the symbol *x*; a group of persons may use the concept *a* or the symbol *x* to denote a common experience they share. In this case, even if the concept is not alienated from the experience, the concept, or the symbol, is only an approximate expression of the experience. This is necessarily so because no person's experience is ever identical with that of another; it can only approximate it sufficiently to permit the use of a common symbol or concept. (In fact, even the experience of one person is never exactly the same on different occasions, because nobody is exactly the same at two different moments of his life.) The concept and the symbol have the great advantage that they permit people to communicate their experiences; they have the tremendous disadvantage that they lend themselves easily to an alienated use.

There is still another factor which contributes to the development of alienation and "ideologization." It seems to be an inherent tendency in human thought to strive for systematization and completeness. (One root for this tendency probably lies in man's quest for certainty—a quest that is understandable enough in view of the precarious nature of human existence.) When we know some fragments of reality we want to complete them in such a way that they "make sense" in a systematic way. Yet by the very nature of the limitations of man we always have only "fragmentary" knowledge, and never complete knowledge. What we tend to do then is to manufacture some additional pieces which we add to the fragments to make of them a whole, a system. Frequently the awareness of the qualitative difference between the "fragments" and "the additions" is missing because of the intensity of the wish for certainty.

This process can frequently be seen even in the development of science. In many scientific systems we find a mixture of true insights into reality, with fictitious pieces added that are intended to produce a systematic whole. Only at a later point of development is it clearly recognized which were the true but fragmentary pieces of knowledge and which the "padding" that was added to give the system greater plausibility. The same process occurs in political ideology. When, in the French Revolution, the French bourgeoisie was fighting for *its own* freedom, it was under the illusion that it was fighting for universal freedom and happiness as absolute principles, and hence applicable to all men.

In the history of religious concepts we find the same process occurring. At the time when man had a fragmentary knowledge of the possibility of solving the problem of human existence by the full development of his human powers; when he sensed that he could find harmony by progressing to the full development of love and reason, rather than by the tragic attempt to regress to nature and to eliminate reason, he gave this new vision, this *x*, many names: Brahman, Tao, Nirvana, God. This development took place all over the world in the millennium between 1500 B.C. and 500 B.C.: * in Egypt, Palestine, India, China, and Greece. The nature of these different concepts depended on the economic, social, and political bases of the respective cultures and social classes, and on the patterns of thought arising from them. But the *x*, the goal, was soon converted into an absolute; a system was built around it; the blank spaces were filled with many fictitious assumptions, until what is common in the vision almost disappeared under the weight of the fictitious "additions" produced by each system.

Any progress in science, in political ideas, in religion and in philosophy tends to create ideologies which compete and fight with each other. Furthermore, this process is aided by the fact that as soon as the thought system becomes the nucleus of an organization, bureaucrats arise who, in order to keep power and control, wish to emphasize the differences rather than that which is shared, and who are therefore interested in making the fictitious additions as important, or more so, than the original fragments. Thus philosophy, re-

* Cf. Karl Jaspers' concept of the "axial age."

ligion, political ideas, and sometimes even science are transformed into ideologies, controlled by the respective bureaucrats.

The concept of God in the Old Testament has its own
life and evolution corresponding to the evolution of a people
within a span of twelve hundred years. There is a common
element of experience referred to by the concept of God,
but there is also a constant change occurring in this experience and hence in the meaning of the word and the concept.
What is common is the idea that neither nature nor artifacts
constitute the ultimate reality or the highest value, but that
there is only the ONE who represents the supreme value and
the supreme goal for man: the goal of finding union with
the world through full development of his specifically human
capacities of love and reason.

The God of Abraham and the God of Isaiah share the
essential qualities of the One, yet they are as different from
each other as are an uneducated, primitive, nomadic tribal
chief and a universalistic thinker living in one of the centers
of world culture a millennium later. There is a growth and
evolution in the concept of God that accompanies the growth
and evolution of a nation; it has a common core, but the
differences that develop in the course of historical evolution
are so great that they often seem to outweigh the common
elements.

In the first stage of this evolution God is visualized as an
absolute ruler. He has made nature and man, and if he is
not pleased with them, he can destroy what he has created.
Yet this absolute power of God over man is counterbalanced
by the idea that man is God's potential rival. Man *could*
become God if only he were to eat from the tree of knowledge *and* from the tree of life. The fruit of the tree of

knowledge gives man God's wisdom; the fruit of the tree of life would give him God's immortality. Encouraged by the serpent, Adam and Eve eat from the tree of knowledge and thus take the first of the two steps. God feels threatened in his supreme position. He says: "Behold, the man has become like one of us, knowing good and evil; and now, lest he put forth his hand and take also of the tree of life, and eat, and live for ever . . ." (Gen. 3:22) To protect himself from this danger God expels man from Paradise and limits his age to not more than one hundred and twenty years.

The Christian interpretation of the story of man's act of disobedience as his "fall" has obscured the clear meaning of the story. The biblical text does not even mention the word "sin"; man challenges the supreme power of God, and he is able to challenge it because he is potentially God. Man's first act is *rebellion,* and God punishes him because he has rebelled and because God wants to preserve his supremacy. God has to protect this supremacy by an act of force, by expelling Adam and Eve from the Garden of Eden and by thus preventing them from taking the second step toward becoming God—eating from the tree of life. Man has to yield to God's superior force, but he does not express regret or repentance. Having been expelled from the Garden of Eden, he begins his independent life; his first act of disobedience is the beginning of human history, because it is the beginning of human freedom.

It is not possible to understand the further evolution of the concept of God unless one understands the contradiction inherent in the early concept. Although he is the supreme ruler, God has created a creature which is his own potential challenger; from the very beginning of his existence, man is the rebel and carries potential Godhood within himself. As we shall see, the more man unfolds, the more he frees himself from God's supremacy, and the more can he become like God.* The whole further evolution of the concept of God diminishes God's role as man's owner.

Once more God appears in the biblical text as the arbitrary ruler who can do with his creatures as the potter may with a vessel that does not please him. Because man is "wicked," God decides to destroy all life on earth.† This story in its continuation, however, leads to the first important change in the concept of God. God "repents" of his decision and decides to save Noah, his family, and every species of animal. But the decisive point here is the fact that God concludes a *covenant* (*berit*), symbolized by the rainbow, with Noah and all his descendants. "I establish my covenant with you, that never again shall all flesh be cut off by the waters of a flood, and never again shall there be a flood to destroy the

---

* Speaking from a historical standpoint, it can be argued that the biblical text is rooted in very old traditions in which God is *not yet* the supreme ruler and in which man represents older deities which are still disputing God's supremacy. While this is likely to be so, it is of no importance from the standpoint of our method of interpretation, which accepts the finally edited text as a unified whole. The editors of the text could have eliminated the archaic passages had they wanted to. But they did not do so, and left it with its inherent contradiction in the picture of God, and hence as a seed for the drastically changed picture of God we find later.

† Considering that this decision follows an archaic sentence dealing with "the sons of the gods" having children "with the daughters of man," one may suspect that man's "wickedness" consists originally in his threat to God's supremacy. The same can be surmised of the story of the Tower of Babel, where God objects to a unified human race, saying "and nothing that they propose to do will now be impossible for them" (Gen. 11:6). To prevent this from happening, God confounds their language and scatters them abroad.

earth" (Gen. 9:11). The idea of the covenant between God and man may have an archaic origin, going back to a time when God was only an idealized man, perhaps not too different from the Olympian gods of the Greeks—a God who resembles man in his virtues and in his vices and who can be challenged by men. But in the context in which the editors of the Bible have put the story of the covenant, its meaning is not that of a regression to more archaic forms of the concept of God but of a progress into a much more developed and mature vision. *The idea of the covenant constitutes, indeed, one of the most decisive steps in the religious development of Judaism,* a step which prepares the way to the concept of the complete freedom of man, even freedom from God.

With the conclusion of the covenant, God ceases to be the absolute ruler. He and man have become partners in a treaty. God is transformed from an "absolute" into a "constitutional" monarch. He is bound, as man is bound, to the conditions of the constitution. God has lost his freedom to be arbitrary, and man has gained the freedom of being able to challenge God in the name of God's own promises, of the principles laid down in the covenant. There is only one stipulation, but it is fundamental: God obliges himself to absolute respect for all life, the life of man and of all other living creatures. The right of all living creatures to live is established as the first law, which not even God can change. It is important to note that the first covenant (in the final editing of the Bible) is one between God and mankind, not between God and the Hebrew tribe. The history of the Hebrews is conceived as only a part of the history of man; the principle of "reverence for life" * precedes all specific promises to one particular tribe or nation.

* Cf. Albert Schweitzer's central thesis.

This first covenant between God and mankind is followed by a second one, between God and the Hebrews.* In Genesis 12:1–3 the covenant is already indicated: "Go from your country and your kindred and your father's house to the land that I will show you. And I will make of you a great nation, and I will bless you, and make your name great, so that you will be a blessing. I will bless those who bless you, and him who curses you I will curse; and by you all the families of the earth will bless themselves." In these last words we find again the expression of universalism. The blessing will not serve Abraham's tribe alone; it is extended to the entire human family. Later, God's promise to Abraham is extended in a covenant that promises his descendants the land between the river of Egypt and the river Euphrates. This covenant is repeated in an extended version in Genesis 17:7–10.

The most dramatic expression of the radical consequences of the covenant is found in Abraham's argument with God when God wants to destroy Sodom and Gomorrah because of their "wickedness." † When God tells Abraham of his plan,

---

* The covenant with Abraham is from the J, the covenant with Noah from the E source, hence the story of the covenant with Abraham would be historically earlier than that with Noah. But in accordance with what has been said in the beginning, this is of no relevance for our analysis. The editor of Genesis has combined the two sources in such a way that the covenant with mankind comes before that with the Hebrew tribe. He had good reasons for doing so, and the book stands as he saw fit.

† The idea of the nature of the sinfulness of Sodom and Gomorrah shows an interesting development in the Jewish tradition. In the biblical text this wickedness is described as homosexuality. This is clearly the meaning of the text, which is also understood in this manner by Rashi, Abraham Ibn Ezra (born 1092), Rashbam (R. Samuel ben Meir, 1085–1174). Nahmanides (R. Moses ben Nachman, 1194–1270), on the other hand, interprets the text as meaning that

Abraham drew near, and said, "Wilt thou indeed destroy the righteous with the wicked? Suppose there are fifty righteous within the city; wilt thou then destroy the place and not spare it for the fifty righteous who are in it? Far be it from thee to do such a thing, to slay the righteous with the wicked, so that the righteous fare as the wicked! Far be that from thee! Shall not the Judge of all the earth do right?" And the Lord said, "If I find at Sodom fifty righteous in the city, I will spare the whole place for their sake." Abraham answered, "Behold, I have taken upon myself to speak to the Lord, I who am but dust and ashes. Suppose five of the fifty righteous are lacking? Wilt thou destroy the whole city for lack of five?" And he said, "I will not destroy it if I find forty-five there." Again he spoke to him, and said, "Suppose forty are found there." He answered, "For the sake of forty I will not do it." Then he said, "Oh, let not the Lord be angry, and I will speak. Suppose thirty are found there." He answered, "I will not do it, if I find thirty there." He said, "Behold, I have taken upon myself to speak to the Lord. Suppose twenty are found there." He answered, "For the sake of twenty I will not destroy it." Then he said, "Oh, let not the Lord be angry, and I will speak again but this once. Suppose ten are found there." He answered, "For the sake of ten I will not destroy it."

Genesis 18:23–32

---

the purpose of the men of Sodom and Gomorrah was to keep strangers away in order to keep all the wealth for themselves. This interpretation is close to the Talmudic definition of the wickedness of Sodom and Gomorrah as being the unwillingness to do something for another which "gives the other pleasure and does not do any harm to oneself."

"Shall not the Judge of all the earth do right?" This sentence marks the fundamental change in the concept of God as the result of the covenant. In courteous language, yet with the daring of a hero, Abraham challenges God to comply with the principles of justice. His is not the attitude of a meek supplicant but that of the proud man who has a right to demand that God uphold the principle of justice. Abraham's language itself moves with consummate artistry between formality and defiance—that is, between the third person singular ("Let the Lord not be angry . . .") and the second person ("Wilt thou destroy the whole city for lack of five?").

With Abraham's challenge a new element has entered the biblical and later Jewish tradition. Precisely because God is bound by the norms of justice and love, man is no longer his slave. Man can challenge God—as God can challenge man—because above both are principles and norms. Adam and Eve challenged God, too, by disobedience; but they had to yield; Abraham challenges God not by disobedience but by accusing him of violating his own promises and principles.* Abraham is not a rebellious Prometheus; he is a free man who has the right to demand, and God has no right to refuse.

The third phase in the evolution of the concept of God is

---

* The question may arise why Abraham stops at the defense of ten just men and does not demand that even for the sake of one man the city must be spared. In my opinion the reason for this lies in the concept that ten men are the minimum constituting a social entity and that Abraham's plea is that God cannot destroy an entire city as long as there is a nucleus that is not wicked. The idea of the nucleus is also to be found in the prophets with regard to Israel and in the Talmudic idea of the "thirty-six just ones," whose existence in each generation is necessary for the survival of mankind.

reached in God's revelation to Moses. Even at this point, however, all anthropomorphic elements have not disappeared. On the contrary, God still "speaks"; he "dwells on a mountain"; he will later write the law on the two tablets. The anthropomorphic language describing God continues throughout the Bible. What is new is that God reveals himself as the God of history rather than the God of nature; most importantly, the distinction between God and an idol finds its full expression in the idea of a *nameless God.*

We shall discuss the story of the liberation from Egypt in some detail later. It will suffice here to mention that in the course of this story God makes repeated concessions to various pleas made by Moses, who states that the pagan Hebrews cannot understand the language of freedom or the idea of a God who reveals himself only as the God of history, without mentioning a name, saying, "I am the God of your father, the God of Abraham, the God of Isaac, and the God of Jacob" (Ex. 3:6). But Moses argues that the Hebrews will not believe him: "Then Moses said to God, 'If I come to the people of Israel and say to them, "The God of your fathers has sent me to you," and they ask me, "What is his name?" what shall I say to them?' " (Ex. 3:13) Moses' objection is well taken. The very essence of an idol is that it has a name; every *thing* has a name because it is complete in time and space. For the Hebrews, accustomed to the concept of idolatry, a nameless God of history could not make sense, for a nameless idol is a contradiction in itself. God recognizes this and makes a concession to the understanding of the Hebrews. He gives himself a name and says to Moses: " 'I AM WHO I AM.' And he said, 'Say this to the people of Israel, "I AM has sent me to you" ' " (Ex. 3:14).

What does this strange name which God gives himself

mean? The Hebrew text says EHEYEH *asher* EHEYEH; or "*Eheyeh* has sent me to you."

Eheyeh is the first person of the imperfect tense of the Hebrew verb "to be." We must remember that in Hebrew there is no present tense but only two basic tense forms: perfect and imperfect. The present can be formed by the use of the participle, as in English "I am writing," but there is no tense corresponding to "I write." All relations of time are expressed by certain secondary alterations to the verb.* Fundamentally an action is experienced as being either perfected or nonperfected. With words denoting actions in the physical world, the perfect necessarily implies the past. If I have perfected writing a letter, my writing is finished; it is in the past. But with activities of a nonphysical nature, like knowing, for instance, it is different. If I have perfected my knowledge, it is not necessarily in the past, but the perfect of knowing can—and often does—mean in Hebrew "I know completely," "I understand thoroughly." The same holds true of verbs like "to love," and the like.†

In considering God's "name," the importance of the *Eheyeh* lies in the fact that it is the imperfect of the verb "to

* Cf. Gesenius, *Hebrew Grammar*, 2nd English ed., revised in accordance with the 28th German ed. (1909) by A. E. Cowley (Oxford: Clarendon Press, 1910), p. 117.

† Psalm 116 is a good example: it starts with the verse *Ahavti ki yishma Adonai et koli tahanunai*. The first word is the perfect of *ahob* (= to love). It means: "I love completely"; then the verse goes on "because the Lord has heard the voice of my prayer." The usual translation "I loved" makes little sense in the context. Although Hebrew grammar was well known to the Christian and Jewish translators of the Bible, they made numerous errors in translating verses such as this one, apparently because they could not free themselves from the sense of time prevailing in the languages of Europe, which have forms to express both time and the quality of perfection.

be." It says God *is*, but his being is not completed like that
of a thing, but is a living process, a becoming; only a thing,
that is, that which has reached its final form, can have a
name. A free translation of God's answer to Moses would be:
"My name is *Nameless*; tell them that 'Nameless' has sent
you." * Only idols have names, because they are things. The
"living" God cannot have a name. In the name of *Eheyeh* we
find an ironical compromise between God's concession to the
ignorance of the people and his insistence that he must be a
nameless God.

This God who manifests himself in history cannot be represented by any kind of image, neither by an image of sound
—that is, a name—nor by an image of stone or wood. This
prohibition of any kind of representation of God is clearly
expressed in the Ten Commandments, which forbid man to
bow down before any "graven image, nor any likeness of
anything that is in heaven above, or that is in the earth beneath, or that is in the water under the earth" (Ex. 20:4).
This command is one of the most fundamental principles of
Jewish "theology."

Though God has been designated by a paradoxical name

---

* The meaning of a nameless God has been beautifully captured by
Master Eckhart. "The final end of being," he said, "is the darkness
of non-knowing of the hidden Godhead, in whom this light shines,
and this darkness did not comprehend it. Hence Moses said: 'He
who hath sent me' (Ex. 3:14). *He who is without a name, and who
never obtained a name*, for which reason the prophet said: 'Truly
thou art a hidden God' (Isaiah 45:14) in the ground of the soul
where God's ground and the soul's are one ground. The more one
seeks Thee, the less one can find Thee. You should seek Him in
such a way as never to find Him. If you do not seek Him, you will
find Him." (James M. Clark, *Meister Eckhart: An Introduction to the
Study of His Works with an Anthology of His Sermons* [Edinburgh:
T. Nelson Sons, 1957], Sermon XXIV, p. 241. [My italics, E.F.]

(YHWH), even this "name" must not be uttered "in vain," it is said in the Ten Commandments. Nahmanides, in his commentary, explains this "in vain" as meaning "to no purpose"; the later Jewish tradition and religious practice has made clear what this "no purpose" means. While observing Jews up to this day never pronounce the YHWH but say instead *Adonai,* which means "my Lord," they will not even say *Adonai* except in prayer or in reading the Scriptures, but substitute for it *Adoshem* (the first letter of Adonai plus the word *shem* which simply means "name") whenever they speak *about* God. Even when writing about God in a foreign language, for instance in English, an observing Jew will write "G'd," in order not to pronounce God's name in vain. In other words, according to Jewish tradition, the biblical prohibition of any kind of representation of God, and against using God's name in vain, means that one can talk *to* God in prayer, in the act of relating oneself *to* God, but one must not talk *about* God lest God be transformed into an idol.* The consequence of this prohibition will be discussed later in this chapter in its reference to the possibility of "theology."

The evolution from the concept of God as a tribal chief to the concept of a nameless God, of whom no representation is permissible, finds its most advanced and radical formulation fifteen hundred years later in the theology of Moses Maimonides. Maimonides (1135–1204) was one of the most outstanding and influential scholars in the rabbinic tradition; he was also the most important Jewish philosopher—or

* It is interesting that in the Jewish tradition there also existed a concept that it was not permissible to make a picture of a person. Inasmuch as God is also in man, man himself in his infinity must not be represented by an image, as a thing.

theologian—of the Middle Ages. In his main philosophical work, *The Guide for the Perplexed,* written in Arabic, he developed his "negative theology," which declares it to be inadmissible to use positive attributes to describe God's *essence* (like existence, life, power, unity, wisdom, will, and so on), although it is permissible to employ attributes of *actions* with regard to God.

Maimonides says: "The wisest man, our Teacher Moses, asked two things of God, and received a reply respecting both. The one thing he asked was that God should let him know His attributes. In answer to both these petitions God promised that He would let him know all His attributes, and that these were nothing but His actions. He also told him that His true essence could not be perceived, and pointed out a method by which he could obtain the utmost knowledge of God possible for man to acquire." *

Maimonides distinguishes between that which ought to be told to ignorant and simple men and what ought to be told to those who have philosophical erudition. To the former, it may suffice to say that they should content themselves that God is One, incorporeal, never subject to external influence, and that he cannot be compared with anything except himself.

But when Maimonides discusses the concept of God for those who are not simple-minded, he concludes that "you must understand that God has no essential attribute in any form or in any sense whatever, and that the rejection of corporeality implies the rejection of essential attributes. Those who believe that God is One, and that He has many attri-

* Moses Maimonides, *The Guide for the Perplexed,* translated from the Arabic by M. Friedländer (London: Pardes Publishing House, 1904), p. 75.

butes, declare the unity with their lips, and assume plurality in their thoughts." *

The conclusion at which Maimonides arrives is the following: "Hence it is clear that He has no positive attribute whatever. The negative attributes, however, are those which are necessary to direct the mind to the truths which we must believe concerning God; for, on the one hand, they do not imply any plurality, and, on the other, they convey to man the highest possible knowledge of God." †

Maimonides' concept that no positive attribute may be used that refers to God's essence leads to an obvious question which he poses in the following form:

The following question might perhaps be asked: Since there is no possibility of obtaining a knowledge of the true essence of God, and since it has also been proved that the only thing that man can apprehend of Him is the fact that He exists, and that all positive attributes are inadmissible, as has been shown; what is the difference among those who have obtained a knowledge of God? Must not the knowledge obtained by our teacher Moses, and by Solomon, be the same as that obtained by any one of the lowest class of philosophers, since there can be no addition to this knowledge? But, on the other hand, it is generally accepted among theologians, and also among philosophers, that there can be a great difference between two persons as regards the knowledge of God obtained by them. Know that this is really the case, that those who have obtained a knowledge of God differ greatly from each other; . . . *It will now be clear to you, that every time you establish by*

* *Ibid.*, p. 67.
† *Ibid.*, p. 82.

*proof the negation of a thing in reference to God, you be-
come more perfect, while with every additional positive
assertion you follow your imagination and recede from
the true knowledge of God.**

Maimonides concludes this discussion by remarking that
Psalm 4:4, "Silence is praise to Thee," expresses best his idea
of the inadequacy of positive attributes.†

As we have seen, there are two interlocking aspects in Maimonides' doctrine of attributes: "the attribute of action, and
the doctrine of negative attributes." ‡ He wants to free the
concept of God from all impurities and does away with all
positive attributes of essence because they imply such impuri-

* *Ibid.*, pp. 83–84. [Italics mine, E.F.]

† The question how he can reconcile his theory with the fact that
the Bible continuously mentions positive attributes of God has been
answered by Maimonides by pointing to the principle "The Torah
speaks in the language of man." He makes these principles even
clearer in his discussion of sacrifice, prayer, and so forth. He points
out that God permitted man to continue some of the accustomed forms
of thought and worship and that he did not command him "to dis-
continue all these manners of services; for to obey such a commandment it would have been contrary to the nature of man, who
generally cleaves to that to which he is used; it would in those days
have made the same impression as a prophet would make at present
if he called us to the service of God and told us in His name that
we should not pray to Him, nor fast, nor seek His help in time of
trouble; that we should serve Him in thought, and not by any
action. For this reason God allowed these kinds of service to
continue; He transferred to His service that which had formerly
served as a worship of created beings, and of things imaginary
and unreal, and commanded us to serve Him in the same manner"
(*Ibid.*, p. 323). The implication here is that prayer, fasting, and
so on are only concessions to man's inclination to cleave to what
he has been used to in the past.

‡ Julius Guttmann, *Philosophies of Judaism*, translated by D. W.
Silverman (New York: Holt, Rinehart and Winston, 1964), p. 161.

ties. Yet he is less radical than the Greek Neoplatonists whose doctrine he followed, because he reintroduces positive attributes to a certain measure, even though not in the formal structure of his thought. Thus, for instance, if we say that God is not impotent we imply that God is omnipotent. And the same holds true of all negations of privations. For this reason Maimonides' theory of negative attributes was objected to during the Middle Ages by philosophers who argued that they "led indirectly to the predication of these very attributes, which, according to Maimonides, should not directly be predicated of God. By denying his [God's] ignorance, we do, in fact, affirm his knowledge; by denying his weakness, we do, in fact, affirm his power." *

As Guttmann sums it up: Maimonides' "doctrine of the negation of privations merely enables us to say that the simple essence of God includes within itself perfections which correspond in one way or another to the qualities of knowledge, will, and power, but whose essence remains undetermined." † While this is an acceptable interpretation, it does not alter the fact that the formal structure of Maimonides' thought is not different from the Greek Neoplatonists in its emphasis on the unknowability of God's essence. Here, as in other aspects of Maimonides, there are certain contradictions which probably have to do with one that exists within Maimonides himself: the bold philosopher, greatly influenced by Greek and Arab thought; and the Talmudic traditionalist rabbi, who did not want to lose touch with the traditional basis of Jewish thought. My own interpretation of Maimonides' theology is based on one aspect of this

* *Ibid.*, p. 164. See Guttmann's discussion of this problem and his reference to Bahya ibn Pakuda, *Book of the Duties of the Heart.*
† *Ibid.*, p. 164.

theology; it seems to me that this is permissible if one does not ignore the fact that actually his position was slightly ambiguous.

The concept of God has gone through a process of evolution starting from the jealous God of Adam, going on to the nameless God of Moses, and continuing to the God of Maimonides, of whom man can know only what he is *not*. The "negative theology" of Maimonides leads, in its ultimate consequence—though one not contemplated by Maimonides —to the end of theology. How can there be a "science of God" when there is nothing one can say or think *about* God? When God himself is the unthinkable, the "hidden," the "silent" God, the Nothing? *

The development from the nameless God of Moses to the God of Maimonides, without attributes of essence, leads to two questions: (1) What is the role of theology in the biblical and later Jewish tradition? (2) What does it mean in this tradition, that man affirms the existence of God?

As to the question about the role of theology † and the development of an orthodoxy, that is, the "right belief," the fact is that neither the Bible nor later Judaism have developed much of a theology. The Bible, of course, abounds with

* Although Maimonides and the mystics are far apart, it is worth remembering that he did make use of non-Aristotelian sources, such as the Neoplatonic systems of al-Farabi and his school, systems which were later taken over by both Jewish and non-Jewish mystics. It is also interesting to note that Maimonides' son Abraham, the author of a number of antirational works which drew on Moslem mysticism, devoted much of his life to a defense of his father's work.

† An excellent discussion of this point is found in Mordecai Kaplan's *Judaism as a Civilization* (New York: Macmillan, 1934). The author refutes brilliantly some of the more extravagant statements that have been made about the nonexistence of a Jewish theology. But, in my opinion, none of his arguments refute the position taken here.

statements about God's actions. He created nature and man; he liberated the Hebrews from Egypt; he led them into the Promised Land. God *is* means God *acts*: with love, compassion, justice, he rewards and punishes. But there are no speculations about the essence and nature of God. That God *is*, is the only theological dogma—if it could be called that —to be found in the Old Testament, and not *what* or *who* God is. In fact, when the Pentateuch says "the hidden mysteries" (*ha-nistaroth*) are not for man to explore, but "that which is open" (Deut. 29:29), it seems to discourage, explicitly, any theological speculation into the nature of God.

Most of the great prophets from Amos onward are equally little concerned with theological speculation. They speak of God's actions, of his commands to man, of his rewards and punishments, but they do not indulge in or encourage any kind of speculation *about* God, just as they do not favor ritual.

At first glance the Talmud and later Jewish tradition seem to contain more of theology and orthodoxy. The most important Talmudic example to be mentioned here, although it is not one dealing with statements about the nature of God, is the insistence of the Pharisees that a pious Jew must believe in the resurrection of the dead (often not clearly differentiated from the immortality of the soul), and the warning that he will have no part in "the world to come" if he does not share in this belief. But a closer examination shows that this rare dogma is a *symptom* of the struggle between two social groups, the Pharisees and the Sadducees, rather than the theological *cause* of the schism between them. The Sadducees represented the aristocracy (secular and priestly), while the Pharisees represented the learned, intellectual sector of the middle classes. Their social and political interests were diametrically opposed, and that carried over to some of their theological views.* The main dogmatic difference between them referred to their views on resurrection. The Pharisees insisted that belief in the resurrection is to be found in the Bible; the Sadducees denied it. The Pharisaic attempt to prove their position consisted of quoting from the Bible. But their citations refute their own view, since the "proofs" they offer consist at best of rather forced interpretations of biblical sentences.† Realistically, the Sadducees were undoubtedly right in maintaining that the Bible does not teach the doctrine of resurrection. From the text in the Mishnah (Sanhedrin X) it is quite clear that the Pharisees wanted to attack the Sadducees by denying them salvation for their disbelief in resurrection as well as for other heresies.‡

* Cf. the brilliant interpretation of this dogmatic difference in Louis Finkelstein, *The Pharisees*, 3rd rev. ed., Vol. II (Philadelphia: The Jewish Publication Society of America, 1962).

† Cf. Sanhedrin 90b. In spite of the official Pharisaic dogma of resurrection, one finds utterances in the Talmud indicating that some of the Talmudic sages were not deeply attached to this belief. Thus, for instance, R. Yohanan, after finishing the Book of Job, used to say: "The end of man is to die and the end of a beast is to be slaughtered, and all are doomed to die. Happy he who was brought up in the Torah and who has given pleasure to his creator and who grew up with a good name and departed the world with a good name! 'A good name is better than precious ointment; and the day of death, than the day of birth [Eccl. 7:1]' " (Berakoth 17a). From my own observations of very observant, learned Jews, I have the impression that quite a few of them believed in the dogma of resurrection, but in a rather abstract way and with little affective weight.

‡ A controversy similar to that with the Sadducees arose several centuries later between the Talmudically oriented sages and the sect of the Karaites. The outstanding Talmudist and philosopher Saadia ha-Gaon disputed the Karaite claim that the Torah and not the "oral tradition" was the only authoritative source of the law.

Aside from this controversy with the Sadducees, little is found in the Talmud that could be described as "theology" and "orthodoxy." What the Talmudic sages mainly argue about are interpretations of the law, the principles governing the conduct of life, but not beliefs about God. The reason for this is that in Jewish tradition belief in God means imitating God's actions, not knowledge *about* him. I stress *about*, because this seems to me the knowledge that one can have only about *things*. It remains true that the prophets and Maimonides speak of the knowledge (*daat*) of God as a first principle, underlying all religious action. But this knowledge is different from a knowledge which would permit using positive attributes of essence about God. The main point I want to make is that "knowing God" in the prophetic sense is the same as loving God or confirming God's existence; it is not speculation about God or his existence; it is not theo-logy.

An interesting illustration is a Talmudic commentary on the accusing sentence of the prophet (Jer. 16:11): "[They] have forsaken me and have not kept my Torah." In *Pesikta de Rav Kahana* we find the comment: "*If only* they had forsaken me and kept my Torah." This commentary, of course, does not mean that its author wanted the Jews to leave God; but it does mean that, given the alternative, it would still be preferable to practice the Torah than to believe in God. The commentators try to soften the harshness of this statement by saying that by keeping the Torah the Jews would eventually return to God.

For the subordinate role of theological dogmas in the later Jewish development, nothing could be more characteristic than the fate of the "thirteen articles of faith" formulated by Maimonides. What happened to these articles? Were they accepted as a dogma or as a belief on which salvation depended? Nothing of the kind. They were never "accepted" or dogmatized—in fact, the most that has been made of them is that in the traditional service of the Ashkenazi Jews they are sung in a poetic version at the end of the evening service of holidays and Sabbaths, and among some Ashkenazi at the conclusion of morning prayers.

The two big schisms which occurred in later Jewish history had little to do with theology proper, though in a broader sense these arguments were conceived as "theological" in the minds of the contestants.* One, after the failure of the false messiah Sabbatai Zevi in the seventeenth century, was the fight against a minority who could not convince themselves that they had been the object of a cruel hoax by a usurper. The other was the schism between Hasidism and their opponents (Mitnagdim), and was the expression of the conflict between the poor and unlearned masses in Galicia, Poland, and Lithuania and the learned rabbis, with their emphasis on intellectual knowledge and learnedness.†

Our discussion of the concept of God has led us to the

---

* There was also a theological clash over Maimonides' work itself when Solomon of Montpellier denounced his writing to the Dominicans, to whom Gregory IX had just given inquisitorial powers. In 1233 his works were publicly burned in Paris. Almost a hundred years later, R. Solomon ben Adret of Barcelona was prevailed upon to issue a ban proscribing the reading of Maimonides by anyone under thirty. (Cf. Joseph Saracheck, *Faith and Reason* [Williamsport, Pa.: The Bayard Press, 1935].) However, the controversy over Maimonides' philosophy did not produce a lasting schism within Judaism.

† In many ways the conflict between Hasidism and its opposition can be compared with that between the *am ha-aretz*, the uneducated peasant, fisherman, or poor artisan of Palestine, from whose ranks Christianity arose, and the learned Pharisees; the social and cultural differences are very much the same in both instances, and also the impatient waiting for the coming of the messiah.

conclusion that in the biblical and later Jewish view there is only one thing that matters, namely, that God *is*. Little importance is attached to the speculation *about* God's nature and essence; hence, there has been no theological development comparable to that which grew up in Christianity. But one can understand the phenomenon that Judaism has not developed an effective theology only if one understands fully that Jewish "theology" was a negative one, not only in the sense of Maimonides, but in still another: *the acknowledgment of God is, fundamentally, the negation of idols.*

Anyone who reads the Hebrew Bible cannot but be impressed by the fact that while it contains hardly any theology, its central issue is the fight against idolatry.

The Ten Commandments, the core of biblical law, while beginning with the declaration, "I am the Lord your God, who brought you out of the land of Egypt, out of the house of bondage" (God is the God of liberation), state as the first commandment the prohibition of idolatry: "You shall have no other gods before me. You shall not make for yourself a graven image, or any likeness of anything that is in heaven above, or that is on the earth beneath, or that is in the water under the earth; you shall not bow down to them or serve them" (Ex. 20:3–6).

The war against idolatry is the main religious theme that runs through the Old Testament from the Pentateuch to Isaiah and Jeremiah. The cruel warfare against the tribes that lived in Canaan, as well as many of the ritual laws, can be understood only as rooted in the desire to protect the people from contamination with idol worship. In the Prophets, the theme of anti-idolatry is no less prominent; but instead of the command to exterminate the idol worshipers, the hope is expressed that all nations will give up idolatry and be united in its common negation.

What is idolatry? What is an idol? Why is the Bible so insistent on uprooting any trace of idolatry? What is the difference between God and idols?

The difference is not primarily that there is only *one* God and *many* idols. Indeed, if man worshiped only one idol and not many, it would still be an idol and not God. In fact, how often has the worship of God been nothing but the worship of one idol, disguised as the God of the Bible?

The approach to the understanding of what an idol is begins with the understanding of *what God is not*. God, as the supreme value and goal, is *not* man, the state, an institution, nature, power, possession, sexual powers, or any artifact made by man. The affirmations "I love God," "I follow God," "I want to become like God"—mean first of all "I do not love, follow, or imitate idols."

An idol represents the object of man's central passion: the desire to return to the soil-mother, the craving for possession, power, fame, and so forth. The passion represented by the idol is, at the same time, the supreme value within man's system of values. Only a history of idolatry could enumerate the hundreds of idols and analyze which human passions and desires they represent. May it suffice to say that the history of mankind up to the present time is primarily the history of idol worship, from the primitive idols of clay and wood to the modern idols of the state, the leader, production and consumption—sanctified by the blessing of an idolized God.

Man transfers his own passions and qualities to the idol. The more he impoverishes himself, the greater and stronger becomes the idol. The idol is the alienated form of man's experience of himself.* In worshiping the idol, man worships himself. But this self is a partial, limited aspect of man: his intelligence, his physical strength, power, fame, and so on. By identifying himself with a partial aspect of himself, man limits himself to this aspect; he loses his totality as a human being and ceases to grow. He is dependent on the idol, since only in submission to the idol does he find the shadow, although not the substance, of himself.

The idol is a *thing*, and it is not alive. God, on the contrary, is a *living* God. "But the Lord is the true God; he is the living God" (Jer. 10:10); or, "My soul thirsts for God, for the living God" (Ps. 42:2). Man, trying to be like God, is an open system, approximating himself to God; man, submitting to idols, is a closed system, becoming a thing himself. The idol is lifeless; God is living. The contradiction between idolatry and the recognition of God is, in the last analysis, that between the love of death and the love of life.†

The idea that the idol is a thing made by man, the work of his hand which he worships and before which he bows down is expressed many times. "Those who lavish gold from the purse," Isaiah says, "and weigh out silver in the scales, hire a goldsmith, and he makes it into a god; then they fall down and worship! They lift it upon their shoulders, they carry it,

---

* The Hegelian-Marxian concept of alienation makes its first appearance—although not in these words—in the biblical concept of idolatry. Idolatry is the worship of the alienated, limited qualities of man. The idolater, just as every alienated man, is the poorer the more richly he endows his idol.

† Cf. E. Fromm, *The Heart of Man* (New York: Harper & Row, 1964.)

they set it in its place, and it stands there; it cannot move from its place. If one cries to it, it does not answer or save him from his trouble" (Is. 46:6–7). The goldsmiths make it a god—a god that cannot move, nor answer, nor respond; a god that is dead; one to whom man can submit, but to whom he cannot relate. There is another forcefully ironical description of the idol by Isaiah:

The ironsmith fashions it and works it over the coals; he shapes it with hammers, and forges it with his strong arm; he becomes hungry and his strength fails, he drinks no water and is faint. The carpenter stretches a line, he marks it out with a pencil; he fashions it with planes, and marks it with a compass; he shapes it into the figure of a man, with the beauty of a man, to dwell in a house. He cuts down cedars; or he chooses a holm tree or an oak and lets it grow strong among the trees of the forest; he plants a cedar and the rain nourishes it. Then it becomes fuel for a man; he takes a part of it and warms himself, he kindles a fire and bakes bread; also he makes a god and worships it, he makes it a graven image and falls down before it. Half of it he burns in the fire; over the half he eats flesh, he roasts meat and is satisfied; also he warms himself and says, "Aha, I am warm, I have seen the fire!" And the rest of it he makes into a god, his idol; and falls down to it and worships it; he prays to it and says, "Deliver me, for thou art my god!" They know not, nor do they discern; for he has shut their eyes, so that they cannot see, and their minds, so that they cannot understand. No one considers, nor is there knowledge or discernment to say, "Half of it I burned in the fire, I also baked bread on its coals, I roasted flesh and have eaten; and shall I make the residue of it an abomination? Shall I fall down before a block of wood?"

Isaiah 44:12–19

Indeed, the nature of idolatry could not be put more drastically: man worships idols that cannot see, and he shuts his eyes so that *he* cannot see.

The same idea is expressed beautifully in Psalm 115: "They [idols] have hands, but do not feel; feet, but do not walk; and they do not make a sound in their throat. Those who make them are like them." In these words the Psalmist expressed the essence of idolatry: the idol is dead, and he who makes it is dead too. It may not be accidental that the author of the psalm, who must have had a keen sense of the love of life, writes a few verses later: "The dead do not praise the Lord, nor do any that go down into silence."

If the idol is the alienated manifestation of man's own powers, and if the way to be in touch with these powers is a submissive attachment to the idol, it follows that idolatry is necessarily incompatible with freedom and independence. Again and again the prophets characterize idolatry as self-castigation and self-humiliation, and the worship of God as self-liberation and liberation from others.* But, one might object, is the Hebrew God not one whom one also fears? This is undoubtedly true as long as God is the arbitrary ruler. But Abraham, while even still afraid, dares to challenge God; and Moses dares to argue with him. Fear of, and submission to, God diminish more and more as the concept of

---

* One might think of the possibility that the original meaning of "awe," which is a blend of "dreadful," as in "awful," and "inspiring," as in "awesome," is derived from the original feeling toward idols, which was a mixture of dread and admiration. The same twofold meaning is found in the corresponding Hebrew word *nora*.

God develops in the course of the later tradition. Man becomes God's partner and almost his equal. God remains, of course, the lawgiver, the one who rewards and punishes; but his rewards and punishments are not arbitrary acts (as, for instance, God's decisions about man's fate in Calvinism); they are the results of man's compliance with, or violation of, the moral law, and not too different from the impersonal Indian karma. God in the Bible and in the later tradition allows man to be free; he reveals to him the goal of human life, the road by which he can reach this goal; but he does not force him to go in either direction. It could hardly be otherwise in a religious system in which, as I shall try to show in the following chapter, the highest norm for man's development is freedom. Idolatry, by its very nature, demands submission —the worship of God, on the other hand, independence.

The logical consequence of Jewish monotheism is the absurdity of theology. If God has no name there is nothing to talk *about*. However, any talk about God—hence all theology—implies using God's name in vain; in fact, it brings one close to the danger of idolatry. On the other hand, idols have names; they are things. They are not *becoming*— they are finished. Hence one can talk about them; one *must* talk about them, because unless one knows them, how can one avoid serving them unwittingly?

Although there is no place for theology, I suggest that there is a place and a need for "idology." The "science of idols" must show the nature of idols and of idolatry, and it must identify the various idols as they have been worshiped during man's history up to, and including, the present time. Once idols were animals, trees, stars, figures of men and women. They were called Baal or Astarte and known by thousands of other names. Today they are called honor, flag, state, mother, family, fame, production, consumption, and many other names. But because the official object of worship is God, the idols of today are not recognized for what they are—the *real* objects of man's worship. Hence we need an "idology" that would examine the *effective* idols of any given period, the kind of worship they have been offered, the sacrifices man has brought them, how they have been syncretized with the worship of God, and how God himself has become one of the idols—in fact, often the highest idol who gives his blessing to the others. Is there really as much difference as we think between the Aztec human sacrifices to their gods and the modern human sacrifices in war to the idols of nationalism and the sovereign state?

The crucial importance of the danger of idolatry has found many expressions in the Jewish tradition. The Talmud, for instance, says: "Whoever denies idolatry is as if he fulfilled the whole Torah" (Hullin 5a). In the later development, concern was expressed that even religious acts might be transformed into idols. Thus one of the great Hasidic masters, the Kozker, said: "The prohibition against the making of idols includes within itself the prohibition against making idols out of the *mitzvot* [religious acts]. We should never imagine that the chief purpose of a *mitzvah* is its outward form, and that its inward meaning should be subordinated. The very opposite is the position we should take." *

"Idology" can show that an alienated man is necessarily an idol worshiper, since he has impoverished himself by transferring his living powers into things outside of himself, which he is forced to worship in order to retain a modicum

* Cf. B. Jeuszohn, quoted by Louis I. Newman, *The Hasidic Anthology* (New York: Charles Scribner's Sons, 1934), p. 193.

of his self, and, in the last analysis, to keep his sense of identity.

The biblical and later Jewish tradition have raised the prohibition of idolatry to a place as high as, or maybe higher than, the worship of God. It is made very clear in this tradition that God can be worshiped only if and when every trace of idolatry has been annulled, not only in the sense that there are no visible and known idols, but also that the attitude of idolatry, submission and alienation, has disappeared.

Indeed, the knowledge of idols and the fight against idolatry can unify men of all religions and those without any religion. Arguments about God will not only divide men but substitute words for the reality of human experience and eventually lead to new forms of idolatry. This does not mean that the adherents of religion should not continue expressing their faith as faith in God (provided they have cleansed their faith of all idolatrous elements) but that mankind can be spiritually united in the negation of idols and thus by an unalienated common faith.

The validity of this interpretation of the role of theology and of the negation of idolatry is borne out by one of the most significant developments in the post-biblical Jewish tradition, the concept of the "Noachites," the sons of Noah.

To understand this idea we must try to understand the peculiar dilemma of the Talmudic sages and their successors. They did not expect, or even want, the other nations of the world to adopt the Jewish faith. On the other hand, the messianic idea implied the eventual unification and salvation of all mankind. Should this mean that in the messianic time all nations would adopt the Jewish faith and be united in the belief in one God?

If so, how can this take place if the Jews refrain from winning proselytes? The answer to this dilemma lies in the concept of the Noachites: "Our rabbis taught: 'Seven precepts were the sons of Noah commanded: social laws to establish courts of justice [or, according to Nahmanides, the principle of social justice], to refrain from blaspheming [cursing the name of God], idolatry, adultery, bloodshed, robbery, and eating flesh from a living animal" (Sanhedrin 56a). The assumption made here is that long before God had revealed himself and given the Torah at Sinai, the generation of Noah was already united by common norms of ethical behavior. Of these norms one refers to the prohibition of an archaic form of eating, namely, eating the flesh from a living animal.* Four precepts refer to the relationship of man to man: the prohibition of bloodshed; robbery; adultery; and the requirement to have a system of law and justice. Only two commandments have a religious content: the prohibition against cursing God's name and that regarding idolatry. The command to worship God is missing.

This in itself does not seem surprising. As long as man had no knowledge of God—how could he have worshiped him? However, the matter is more complicated; if he had no knowledge of God, how could he even be commanded not to curse him and not to worship idols? Historically, referring to the generation of Noah, these two negative prohibitions hardly make any sense.† But if one takes the Talmudic

* The essential point here seems to be the same as in the later prohibition in regard to eating the blood of an animal, because "blood is life." Man must refrain from consuming life.

† H. Cohen has pointed out that Joh. Selden, *De Jure Naturali et Gentium Justa Disciplinam Ebraeorum* (London, 1890), already saw the significance of the concept of the Noachites for natural and international law. The same was emphasized by A. G. Waehner

statement not as a historical truth but as an ethical-religious concept, then we see that the rabbis formulated a principle in which "negative theology" (in a different sense than that of Maimonides), namely, *not* to blaspheme and *not* to worship idols, is all that was required of the sons of Noah. This particular Talmudic quotation says only that the two negative commands have their validity for the time before the revelation of God to Abraham, and it does not exclude the possibility that after this event the worship of God is a valid norm for all people. But another concept found in rabbinical literature, that of the "pious of the peoples of the world," the pious Gentiles (*hasidei umoth ha-olam*), indicates that this is not the case. This group is defined as those who fulfill the seven precepts of Noah. The essential point in this new concept is that it is said of them: "The righteous among the Gentiles have their place in the world to come" (Tosefta, Sanhedrin, XIII,2). This "place in the world to come" is the traditional term for salvation, customarily used in reference to all Jews living in accordance with the commandments of the Torah. The legal formulation is in Maimonides, *Mishneh Torah*, XIV,5,8: "A heathen who accepts the seven commandments [of Noah] and observes them scrupulously is a 'righteous heathen' and will have a portion in the world to come."

What does this concept ultimately imply? Mankind, for its salvation, does not need to worship God. All it needs is *not* to blaspheme God and *not* to worship idols. Thus the sages solved the conflict between the messianic idea that all

---

in his *Antiquitates Ebraeorum* (1743). Hugo Grotius also praised the concept of the Noachites. Cf. H. Cohen, *Die Religion der Vernunft aus den Quellen des Judentums* (Frankfurt: J. Kaufman Verlag, 1929), p. 143.

men will be saved and their aversion to making proselytes. Universal salvation is not dependent on adherence to Judaism; it is not even dependent on the worship of God. The human race will have achieved the condition of blessedness, providing only that it does not worship idols and does not blaspheme God. This is the *practical* application of "negative theology" to the problem of the salvation and the unity of the human race. If mankind has achieved solidarity and peace, not even the common worship of one God is necessary.*

But is it not illogical that those who do not believe in God should be prohibited from cursing him? Why should it be a virtue not to curse God if I do not believe in him? It seems to me that this obvious objection oversimplifies matters by taking the statements too literally. From the standpoint of the biblical and post-biblical tradition, there is no doubt that God exists. If a man blasphemes God, he attacks that which is symbolized by the concept of God. If he simply does not worship God, from the viewpoint of the believer this may be due to ignorance and not imply a positive attack on the concept of God. We must also remember that in the Jewish tradition, to curse God has the special meaning of violating a powerful taboo. Not cursing God, in my opinion, is parallel to not worshiping idols; in both cases a man avoids positive error, even though to the theist he has not fully grasped the truth.

We have seen that in the Jewish tradition the imitation of God's actions has replaced the knowledge of God's essence.

---

* The subject of the Noachites, which has been dealt with here in connection with the problem of "negative theology," has been masterfully handled by Hermann Cohen in connection with love for the stranger in his *Die Religion der Vernunft.*

It must be added that God acts in history and reveals himself in history. This idea has two consequences: one, that belief in God implies a concern with history and, using the word in its widest sense, a *political* concern. We see this political concern most clearly in the prophets. Quite in contrast to the Far Eastern masters, the prophets think in historical and political terms. "Political" here means that they are concerned with historical events affecting not only Israel but all the nations of the world. It means, furthermore, that the criteria for judging historical events are spiritual-religious ones: justice and love. According to these criteria nations are judged, as are individuals, by their actions.

We have seen that for historical reasons the Jews have given the name "God" to the *x*, which man should approximate in order to be fully man. They developed their thought to the point where God ceases to be definable by any positive attributes of essence, and where the right way of living —for individuals and for nations—takes the place of theology. Although logically the next step in the Jewish development would be a system without "God," it is impossible for a theistic-religious system to take this step without losing its identity. Those who cannot accept the concept of God find themselves outside the system of concepts that makes up the Jewish religion. They might, however, be quite close to the spirit of the Jewish tradition, provided they make the task of "right living" the foremost goal of life, although this "right living" would not be the fulfillment of the rituals and of many specifically Jewish commandments, but acting in the spirit of justice and love within the frame of reference of modern life. They will find themselves close to the Buddhists, and to those Christians who, like Abbé Pire, say: "What matters today is not the difference between believers and nonbelievers, but that between those who care and those who do not care."

Before concluding this chapter another question must be faced, which may already have arisen in the minds of many readers. If I define as the essence of a Jewish religious system the *imitatio dei* instead of theology, am I not suggesting that Judaism is essentially an ethical system which demands from men that they act justly, truthfully, and compassionately? Is Judaism an ethical, rather than a religious, system?

There are two answers to this question. The first is found in the concept of the *halakhah* * that man must act not only according to general principles of justice, truth, and love, but that every act of life be "sanctified," becoming imbued with a religious spirit. "Right action" refers to everything: to the prayer in the morning, to the benediction over food, to the sight of the ocean and of the first flower of the season, to helping the poor, to visiting the sick, to not making a man ashamed in the presence of others.

But even this understanding of *halakhah* could be taken to imply simply a very extended system of "ethical culture." The question still remains whether Judaism, despite its strong emphasis on global ethics, is more than an ethical system.

Before we can discuss the difference between the ethical (good) man and the religious man, the problem of ethics needs some further clarification. It is important to distinguish between an "authoritarian" and a "humanistic" ethics.† An

---

* To be discussed in detail in Chapter V.

† Cf. the detailed discussion of these concepts in E. Fromm, *Man for Himself* (New York: Holt, Rinehart and Winston, 1947), Chap. IV.

authoritarian conscience (Freud's superego) is the voice of an internalized authority, such as parents, state, religion. "Internalized" means that a person has made the rules and prohibitions of the authority his own and obeys them as if he were obeying himself; he experiences this voice as his own conscience. This type of conscience, which may also be called heteronomous conscience, guarantees that the person can be relied upon to act always according to the demands of his conscience; but it becomes dangerous when the authorities command evil things. The person with the "authoritarian conscience" considers it his duty to comply with the commands of the authorities to whom he submits, regardless of their content; indeed, there is no crime which has not been committed in the name of duty and conscience.

Quite different from the authoritarian (heteronomous) conscience is the "humanistic" (autonomous) conscience. It is not the internalized voice of an authority whom we are eager to please and afraid of displeasing; it is the voice of our total personality expressing the demands of life and growth. "Good" for the humanistic conscience is all that furthers life; "evil" is all that arrests and strangles it. The humanistic conscience is the voice of our self which summons us back to ourselves, to *become* what we potentially are.* The person whose conscience is essentially autonomous † does the right things not by forcing himself to obey the voice of the internalized authority, but because he *enjoys* doing what is right, even though often he will need some practice in following his principles before he can fully enjoy his action.

* Cf. a detailed discussion in E. Fromm, *The Heart of Man* (New York: Harper & Row, 1964).

† Needless to say that in reality we find mostly blends between these two types of conscience; what matters is the respective weight of each type in the entire conscience.

He does not do his "duty" (from *debere* = to owe) by obeying an authority, but he is "responsible" because he "responds" (from *respondere* = to answer) to the world of which he is a part as an alive, inwardly active human being.

When we speak of the "ethical" attitude in comparison with a "religious" attitude, therefore, it matters a great deal whether we are talking of primarily authoritarian or of humanistic ethics. Authoritarian ethics are always tinged by idolatry. I act in accordance with the orders of an authority whom I worship as the possessor of the absolute judgment of right and wrong; authoritarian ethics are, by their very nature, alienated ethics. They represent an attitude which in many respects contradicts that of the religious person, in the sense described in the following pages. The attitude of humanistic ethics is not alienated or idolatrous. Hence they are not contrary to the religious attitude. This does not mean, however, that there is no difference.

Assuming that the attitude underlying the Jewish tradition transcends the ethical realm, the problem arises as to what its particular religious element is. It would be simple to answer that this element consists of belief in God, in a supernatural, supreme Being. According to this view a religious man would be a believer in God who is at the same time (and as a consequence of his belief) an ethical man. Such a definition, however, raises many questions. Is the quality of the religious * not founded here entirely on a *thought* concept, God? Does it follow that a Zen Buddhist or the "pious among the Gentiles" cannot be called religious?

At this point we arrive at a central question. Is religious experience necessarily connected with a theistic concept? I

---

* It is worth while to note that classical Hebrew has no equivalent for "religion" or "religious." Medieval and modern Hebrew uses a word (*dat*) from an Arabic root.

believe not; one can describe a "religious" experience as a human experience which underlies, and is common to, certain types of theistic, as well as nontheistic, atheistic, or even antitheistic conceptualizations. What differs is the conceptualization of the experience, not the experiential substratum underlying various conceptualizations. This type of experience is most clearly expressed in Christian, Moslem, and Jewish mysticism, as well as in Zen Buddhism. If one analyzes the experience rather than the conceptualization, therefore, one can speak of a *theistic as well as of a nontheistic religious experience.*

There remains the epistemological difficulty. There is no word for the substratum of this type of religious experience in Western languages, except when it is referred to in connection with theism. Hence it is ambiguous to use the word "religious"; even the word "spiritual" is not much better, since it has other misleading connotations. For these reasons I think it is preferable to speak, at least in this book, of the *x experience,** which is found in religious and in philosophical systems (such as that of Spinoza), regardless of whether they do or do not have a concept of God.

A psychological analysis of the *x* experience would go far beyond the scope of this book. However, in order to indicate

---

* The question of a nontheistic religious experience has been widely discussed in recent years by Protestant theologians. Paul Tillich used the concept "ground of being," or simply "depth," as a substitute for God. Professor Altizer has spoken of atheistic Christianity; Dietrich Bonhoeffer, of nonreligious Christianity. The Bishop of Woolwich, John A. T. Robinson, has expressed views in the same direction in his *Honest to God* (London: S.C.M. Press, 1963). Cf. also Paul Tillich, *The Shaking of the Foundation* and *Systematic Theology*; Rudolf Bultmann in *Kerygma and Myth*; Dietrich Bonhoeffer in his *Letters from Prison*; and D. T. Suzuki in *Mysticism, East and West*, which shows the essential identity between Western theistic and Eastern nontheistic mystical attitudes.

briefly at least some of the main aspects of the phenomenon,
I suggest the following points:

(1) The first characteristic element is *to experience life
as a problem*, as a "question" that requires an answer. The
non-*x* person does not feel a deep, or at least not a conscious,
disquiet about the existential dichotomies of life. Life as
such is not a problem for him; he is not bothered by the need
for a solution. He is—at least consciously—satisfied with
finding the meaning of life in work or pleasure or power
or fame or even, like the ethical man, in acting in accordance
with his conscience. To him mundane life makes sense, and
he does not experience the pain of his separateness from man
and nature nor the passionate wish to overcome this separateness and to find at-one-ment.

(2) For the *x* experience there exists a definite hierarchy
of values. The highest value is the optimal development of
one's own powers of reason, love, compassion, courage. All
worldly achievements are subordinated to these highest
human (or spiritual, or *x*) values. This hierarchy of values
does not imply asceticism; it does not exclude worldly
pleasures and joys, but it makes the worldly life part of the
spiritual life; or rather, the worldly life is permeated by the
spiritual aims.

(3) Related to the hierarchy of values is another aspect of
the *x* experience. For the average person, especially in a
materialistic culture, life is a means toward ends other than
the person himself. These ends are: pleasure, money, power,
the production and distribution of commodities, and so on.
If man is not used by others for their ends, he uses himself
for his own; in both cases he becomes a means. For the *x*
person, man alone is an end and never a means. Furthermore,
his whole attitude toward life is one in which each event is
responded to from the standpoint of whether or not it helps

to transform him in the direction of becoming more human. Whether it is art or science, joy or sorrow, work or play, whatever happens is a stimulus to his becoming stronger and more sensitive. This process of constant inner transformation and of becoming part of the world in the act of living is the aim toward which all other aims are subordinated. Man is not a subject opposing the world in order to transform *it*; he is *in* the world making his being in the world the occasion for constant self-transformation. Hence the world (man and nature) is not an object standing opposite to him, but the medium in which he discovers his own reality and that of the world ever more deeply. Neither is he a "subject," the least indivisible part of human substance (an atom, an individual), not even Descartes' lofty thinking subject, but a self that is alive and strong precisely to the degree to which it ceases to hold onto itself, but *is* by responding.

(4) More specifically, the *x* attitude can be described in the following terms: a letting go of one's "ego," one's greed, and with it, of one's fears; a giving up the wish to hold onto the "ego" as if it were an indestructible, separate entity; a making oneself empty in order to be able to fill oneself with the world, to respond to it, to become one with it, to love it. To make oneself empty does not express passivity but *openness*. Indeed, if one cannot make oneself empty, how can one respond to the world? How can one see, hear, feel, love, if one is filled with one's ego, if one is driven by greed? *

* This kind of emptiness is quite different from what the psychoanalyst would call "receptiveness." The latter is passive; emptiness is active—just as inhaling is as active as exhaling. Cf. the excellent *Metamorphosis* by Ernest Schachtel (New York: Basic Books, 1959), with regard to the problem of activity and passivity.

(5) The *x* experience can also be called one of transcendence. But here again we find the same problem as in the case of the word "religious." "Transcendence" is conventionally used in the sense of God's transcendence. But as a human phenomenon we deal with transcending the ego, leaving the prison of one's selfishness and separateness; whether we conceive of this transcendence as one toward God is a matter of conceptualization. The experience is essentially the same whether it refers to God or not.

The *x* experience, whether theistic or not, is characterized by the reduction, and, in its fullest form, by the disappearance, of narcissism. In order to be open to the world, to transcend my ego, I must be able to reduce or to give up my narcissism. I must, furthermore, give up all forms of incestuous fixation and of greed; I must overcome my destructiveness and necrophilous tendencies. I must be able to love life. I must also have a criterion for differentiating between a false *x* experience, rooted in hysteria and other forms of mental illness, and the nonpathological experience of love and union. I must have a concept of true independence, must be able to differentiate between rational and irrational authority, between idea and ideology, between willingness to suffer for my convictions and masochism.*

It follows from all the foregoing considerations that the analysis of the *x* experience moves from the level of theology to that of psychology and, especially, psychoanalysis. First of all, because it is necessary to differentiate between conscious

* Cf. E. Fromm, *The Heart of Man*, in which I have analyzed these phenomena in detail, especially the syndrome of evil (or decay); necrophilia (love of death); symbiotic, incestuous fixation, and malignant narcissism. It is interesting to note that Maimonides postulated physical and mental health as requirements for a prophet.

thought and affective experience which may or may not be expressed in adequate conceptualizations. Secondly, because psychoanalytic theory permits an understanding of those unconscious experiences which underly the x experience or, on the other hand, those which are opposed to it or block it. Without an understanding of unconscious processes, it is difficult to appreciate the relative and often accidental character of our conscious thoughts. However, in order to understand the x experience, psychoanalysis must enlarge its conceptual frame beyond that outlined by Freud. The central problem of man is not that of his libido; it is that of dichotomies inherent in his existence, his separateness, alienation, suffering, his fear of freedom, his wish for union, his capacity for hate and destruction, his capacity for love and union.

In short, we are in need of an empirical psychological anthropology which studies x and non-x experience as experiential human phenomena, regardless of conceptualizations. Such a study might lead to establishing rationally the superiority of the x way to all others, as methodologically the Buddha already did. It may occur that while the Middle Ages were concerned with the proof of God's existence with philosophical and logical arguments, the future will be concerned with outlining the essential rightness of the x way on the basis of a highly developed anthropology.

Summing up the main line of thought of this chapter: the idea of the One God expresses a new answer for the solution of the dichotomies of human existence; man can find oneness with the world, not by regressing to the prehuman state, but by the full development of his specifically human qualities: love and reason. The worship of God is first of all the negation of idolatry. The concept of God is at first formed according to the political and social concepts of a tribal chief or king. The image is then developed of a constitutional monarch who is obligated to man to abide by his own principles: love and justice. He becomes the nameless God, the God about whom no attribute of essence can be predicated. This God without attributes, who is worshiped "in silence," has ceased to be an authoritarian God; man must become fully independent, and that means independent even from God. In "negative theology," as well as in mysticism, we find the same revolutionary spirit of freedom which characterized the God of the revolution against Egypt. I could not express this spirit better than by quoting Master Eckhart:

> That I am a man
> I have in common with all men,
> That I see and hear
> And eat and drink
> I share with all animals.
> But that I am I is exclusively mine,
> And belongs to me
> And to nobody else,
> To no other man
> Nor to an angel nor to God,
> Except inasmuch as I am one with him.*

* *Fragments.* [My translation, E.F.]

iii *The Concept of*

MAN

The most fundamental statement of the Bible in regard to the nature of man is that man is made in the image of God. "Then God said, 'Let us make man in our image, after our likeness; and let them have dominion over the fish of the sea, and over the birds of the air, and over the cattle, and over all the earth, and over every creeping thing that creeps upon the earth.' So God created man in his own image, in the image of God he created him; male and female he created them" (Gen. 1:26–27).* There is no question about

---

* The Jewish sages found some difficulty in explaining the use of the plural in the sentence "Let us make man . . ." where, contrary to the general pattern the subject, God (*Elohim*), which is itself a

the emphasis the story puts on this point. It uses two expressions, "image" and "likeness," and then again repeats in the
next verse the same idea. The biblical report not only speaks
of man being made in the image of God—it expresses shortly
afterward God's fear that man might become God himself.
This fear is clearly stated in Gen. 3:22–23. Man has eaten
from the tree of knowledge; he has not died, as the serpent
had correctly predicted; he has become *as* God. Only mor-
tality distinguishes him from God. Made in the image of
God, being *as* God, he *is not* God. To prevent that from
happening, God expels Adam and Eve from Paradise. The
serpent, who had said *eritis sicut dei* ("you shall be like
gods") had been right.

That man could become God, and that God prevents him
from attaining this goal, is probably an archaic part of the
text. Yet it has not been eliminated by the various editors,
and they must have had their reasons for this. Perhaps one

---

plural, is connected with the plural form of the verb "Let us make"
(*naaseh*). Naturally they wanted to refute any suspicion that the idea
of the unity of God could be questioned in this formulation. Rashi's
comment is: "This teaches us God's humility; because man was made
in the likeness of the angels, He first consulted them, notwithstanding
that this might be taken to mean that He made man with their assist-
ance. Scripture thereby informs us that the greater should always consult and receive permission of the lesser." Rashi's idea that God consulted the angels is surprising if we consider that it is quite contrary to
the spirit of the biblical story in which God certainly is represented as
an autocratic ruler who does not consult anybody. But Rashi gives expression here to the much later development, when God is no longer
the autocratic ruler, and which we find in statements saying that God
consults man in regard to the government of the world (cf. Sanhedrin
38b). In the older (J) version of man's creation, the idea of man's
being created in God's image is missing. It says: "Then the Lord God
formed man of dust from the ground, and breathed into his nostrils
the breath of life; and man became a living being" (Gen. 2.7).

reason is that they wanted to emphasize that man is not God, nor could he become God; he can become *like* God, he can imitate God, as it were. Indeed, this idea of the *imitatio Dei,* of approximating God, requires the premise that man is made in God's image.

In the Bible this concept of the approximation of God is expressed in the statement: "And the Lord said to Moses, 'Say to all the congregation of the people of Israel, You shall be holy; for I the Lord your God am holy' " (Lev. 19:1-2).* If we consider that the concept "holy" (*kadosh*) expresses that essential quality of God which separates him from man, that which in the primitive stages of religion made God taboo and unapproachable, it becomes clear what an important step of development is marked by the phrase that man can also be "holy." † In the prophets, from Amos onward, we find the same concept. What man is to do is to acquire and to practice the main qualities that characterize God: justice and love (*rahamim*). Micah

---

* Cf. the discussion of Maimonides' negative theology which refers to the attributes of being, not to those of action. We see the beginning of this attitude already in the Talmud in the following story: "A certain [reader] went down in the presence of R. Hanina and said: 'O God, the great, mighty, terrible, majestic, powerful, awful, strong, fearless, sure, and honored.' He [R. Hanina] waited till he had finished, and when he had finished he said to him, 'Have you concluded all the praise of your Master? Why do we want all this? Even with these three that we do say [great, mighty, and terrible—in the first benediction], had not Moses our master mentioned them in the Law, and had not the men of the great Synagogue come and inserted them in the Tefillah, we should not have been able to mention them' " (Berakhot 33b).

† Cf. The comments on *kadosh* in Harris H. Hirschberg, *Hebrew Humanism* (Los Angeles, Cal.: California Writers, 1964). This book is an excellent and profound presentation of many problems of Hebrew humanism.

formulated this principle succinctly: "He has showed you, O man, what is good; and what does the Lord require of you but to do justice, and to love kindness [or steadfast love], and to walk humbly with your God?" (Micah 6:8) In this formulation we find another picture of the relationship between God and man. Man is not God, but if he acquires God's qualities, he is not beneath God, but walks *with* him.

The same idea of the imitation of God is continued in the rabbinical literature of the first centuries after the destruction of the Temple. " 'To walk in all his ways' (Deut. 11:22) . . . which are God's ways? As it says (Ex. 34:6), 'The Lord, the Lord, God merciful (*rahum* = loving) and gracious, long suffering and abundant in goodness and truth; keeping mercy until the thousandth generation, forgiving iniquity and transgression and sin and He clears away (sin) '; and it says (Joel 2:32) 'And it shall come to pass that whosoever shall call (himself) by the name of the Lord, shall be delivered.' But how is it possible for man to call (himself) by the name of the Lord? Just as God is called merciful and gracious, be also thou merciful and gracious, and give gifts to anybody without expecting a return; as God is called righteous . . . be also thou righteous; as God is called loving, be also thou loving." *

As Hermann Cohen has pointed out, the qualities of God (*midot*), enumerated in Exodus 34:6,7, have been trans-

---

* Sifre Deut. 11, 22, 49, 85a, quoted by A. Buechler, *Studies in Sin and Atonement in the Rabbinic Literature of the First Century* (London: Oxford University Press, 1928), pp. 35f. Buechler translates the Hebrew *hasid* of the text as "loving"; the more conventional translation would be "pious."

formed into *norms* for human action. "Only the *effects* of
his essence," says Cohen, "does God want to reveal to
Moses, not his essence itself." *

How does man try to imitate God's actions?
By practicing the commandments of God, his "law." As
I shall try to show in a later chapter, what is called God's
law consists of many parts. One part, which constitutes the
center of prophetic teaching, is made up of the rules of
action which express and bring about love and justice.
To free those who are in chains, to feed the hungry, to
help the helpless, are the ever-repeated norms of right
action which the prophets preach. The Bible and the
rabbinical tradition have implemented these general norms
by hundreds of specific laws, from the biblical prohibition
against charging interest on a loan to the rabbinical command to visit the sick, yet not to visit a sick enemy, since
he might feel embarrassed.

This imitation of God by acting the way God acts means
becoming more and more like God; it means at the same
time *knowing* God. "Accordingly, to know the ways of God
means to know and to follow in practice His dealings with
men, His all-embracing principles of justice, unlimited love,
loving-kindness and forgiveness." †

In the tradition from the Bible to Maimonides, knowing
God and being like God means to imitate God's actions
and not to know or speculate about God's essence. As
Hermann Cohen puts it: "The place of being is taken by
action; the place of causality is taken by purpose." ‡
Theology, we might also say, is replaced by the study of the

---

* H. Cohen, *op. cit.*, p. 110. [My italics, E.F.]
† A. Buechler, *op. cit.*, p. 358.
‡ H. Cohen, *op. cit.*, p. 109.

law; speculation about God by practice of the law. This also explains why the study of the Bible and Talmud has been made into one of the most important religious duties.

The same idea is expressed in a rabbinical concept that says that the violation of the law means the denial of God. Thus we read: "Hence you can learn that they who lend money for interest *Kofrin beikar*, deny the 'fundamental principle.' " * What holds true of taking interest, holds true of lying. Thus R. Haninah ben Hakhinai comments on Leviticus 5:21 ("If a soul lie unto his neighbour") by saying: "No one lies to his neighbour without denying 'the fundamental principle.' " † As Buechler points out, "The Creator," the "fundamental principle," and the giver of the Commandments are synonymous with God.‡

What we have described so far represents the main line of biblical and rabbinical thought: man can become *like* God, but he cannot become God. But it is certainly worth noting that there are rabbinical statements that imply that the difference between God and man can be eliminated. A statement expressing the idea that man can become the creator of life, as God is, is to be found in the following: "Raba said: If the righteous desired it, they could [by living a life of absolute purity] be creators, for it is written: 'but your iniquities have distinguished between . . .' " (Is. 59:2) [Raba understands *mavedilim* in the sense of "draw a distinction." But for their iniquities, their power would equal God's and they could create a world.] Raba created a man and sent him to R. Zera. R. Zera spoke to him, but received no answer. Therefore he said unto him:

* Tosefta Baba Meztia. 6,17; quoted by A. Buechler, *op. cit.*, p. 104.
† Tosefta Shebuoth 3,6; quoted by A. Buechler, *op. cit.*, p. 105.
‡ A. Buechler, *ibid.*, p. 105.

"Thou art a creature of the magicians. Return to the dust" (Sanhedrin 65b).

Another Talmudic saying speaks of man not as able to *be* God but to be God's equal, sharing with him the ruler- ship over the world. Interpreting the verse from Daniel which speaks of "thrones," the Talmud says: "One [throne] was for himself and one for David [the messiah]: this is R. Akiba's view. R. Jose protested to him: How long wilt thou profane the Shekinah [an aspect of God, by asserting that a human being sits beside him]" (Sanhedrin 38b). While it is later argued that R. Akiba interpreted the two thrones as being those of mercy and justice respectively, the view ascribed to one of the greatest figures of Judaism that a *man* sits on a throne beside God is of great importance, even though R. Akiba does not represent the traditional view in his statement. Here man (for in the Jewish tradition the messiah is man, and nothing but man) governs the world together with God.*

It is obvious that neither R. Akiba's view that the messiah sits on a throne beside God nor Raba's view that if only man were entirely pure he could create life, like God, are in any way official views of Judaism. But the very fact that two of the greatest rabbinical masters could express such "blasphemies" shows the existence of a tradition re- lated to the main current of Jewish thought: man, though being mortal and beset by the conflict between his godly and his earthly aspects, nevertheless is an open system and can develop to the point of sharing God's power and

---

* One might surmise that the tradition in which R. Akiba's state- ment is rooted underlies the heterodox Christian adoptionist concept of Christ and man being *adopted* by God, sitting at the right hand of God. In the Jewish tradition there is no adoption.

capacity for creation. This tradition has found a beautiful expression in Psalm 8: "Thou has made him [man] little lower than God [or gods, or the angels; in Hebrew *elohim*]."

Man is seen as being created in God's likeness, with a capacity for an evolution of which the limits are not set. "God," a Hasidic master remarked, "does not say that 'it was good' after creating man; this indicates that while the cattle and everything else were finished after being created, man was not finished." It is man himself, guided by God's word as voiced by the Torah and the Prophets, who can develop his inherent nature in the process of history.

What is the nature of this human evolution?

Its essence lies in man's emergence from the incestuous * ties to blood and soil into independence and freedom. Man, the prisoner of nature, becomes free by becoming fully human. In the biblical and later Jewish view, freedom and independence are the goals of human development, and the aim of human action is the constant process of liberating oneself from the shackles that bind man to the past, to nature, to the clan, to idols.

Adam and Eve at the beginning of their evolution are bound to blood and soil; they are still "blind." But "their eyes are opened" after they acquire the knowledge of good and evil. With this knowledge the original harmony with nature is broken. Man begins the process of individuation and cuts his ties with nature. In fact, he and nature become enemies, not to be reconciled until man has become fully human. With this first step of severing the ties between man and nature, history—and alienation—begins. As we

---

* By "incestuous," I mean not primarily a sexual but essentially an affective tie to mother and nature.

have seen, this is not the story of the "fall" of man but of
his awakening, and thus, of the beginning of his rise.

But even before the story of the expulsion from Paradise
(which is a symbol of the mother's womb), the biblical text
—using nonsymbolic language—proclaims the necessity of
cutting the bond to father and mother: "Therefore a man
leaves his father and his mother and cleaves to his wife, and
they become one flesh" (Gen. 2:24). The meaning of this
verse is quite clear: the condition for man's union with
woman is that he shall cut the primary ties to his parents,
that he shall become an independent man. Love between
man and woman is possible only when the incestuous tie
has been severed. (Rashi also interprets this verse as implying the prohibition of incest.)

The next step in the process of liberation from incestuous
ties is found in the beginning of the national history of the
Hebrews. Abraham is told by God to cut the ties with
his father's house, to leave it, and to go into a country which
God will show him. The Hebrew tribes, after long wanderings, settle in Egypt. A new dimension is added—the social
one of slavery—to the ties of blood and soil. Man must cut
not only the tie to father and mother; he must also cut the
social ties which make him a slave, dependent on a master.

The idea that man's task lies in the growing emancipation
from the "primary ties" * of incestuous attachment is also
expressed in some of the main religious symbols and services
of the Jewish tradition: Passover, Sukkoth, and the Sabbath.
Passover is the celebration of the liberation from slavery,
and as the *Haggadah* says, every person must feel as if he
himself had been a slave in Egypt and had been liberated

* Cf. E. Fromm, *Escape from Freedom* (New York: Holt, Rinehart
and Winston, 1941).

from there. The *matzot,* or unleavened bread, which is eaten during the week of Passover, is a symbol of wandering: it is the bread baked by the Hebrews when they had no time to use leaven. The *sukkah* (the tabernacle) has the same symbolic meaning. It is a "temporary abode" instead of the "permanent abode"; by living (or at least eating) in the "temporary abode" the Jew makes himself again a wanderer, whether he lives on the soil of Palestine or whether he is in the Diaspora. Both the *matzot* and the *sukkah* symbolize the cutting of the umbilical cord to the soil. (The Sabbath, as the anticipation of complete freedom, will be discussed in a later chapter.)

Against our thesis that the Jewish aim for man is independence and freedom, the objection may be raised that the Bible, as also the later tradition, requires obedience to the father, and that in the Old Testament the rebellious son is severely punished. It is perfectly true that the Hebrew Bible is permeated by an emphasis on obedience, but it must be noted that obedience is quite different from incestuous fixation.

Obedience is a conscious act of submitting to authority; in this respect obedience is the opposite of independence. Fixation is an *emotional* tie to a person binding one affectively to that person. Obedience is usually conscious; it is behavior rather than feeling, and it can occur also when the feelings toward the authority are hostile, and when the person obeys without agreeing with the authority's orders. Fixation as such is usually unconscious; what is conscious is a feeling of love or fear. The obedient person is afraid of punishment if he disobeys. The fixated person is afraid of being lost and cast out if he tries to sever the incestuous tie. Historically, obedience is usually obedience to the father;

fixation is the tie to the mother, in extreme cases the "symbiotic" tie that blocks the process of individuation. While in patriarchal societies the fear of the father is more obvious, fright of the mother is more deep, and its intensity depends on the intensity of the fixation to her.

The distinction between incestuous fixation and obedience to authority requires further clarification. By incestuous fixation we have understood fixation to mother, to blood, and to soil.* Incestuous fixation is by its very nature a bond with the past and a hindrance to full development. Obedience in the patriarchal world of the biblical and later Jewish tradition is obedience to the father figure who represents reason, conscience, law, moral and spiritual principles. The highest authority in the biblical system is God, who is the lawgiver and who represents conscience. In the process of the development of the human race, there was perhaps no other way to help man liberate himself from the incestuous ties to nature and clan than by requiring him to be obedient to God and his laws.

A further step in man's development enables him to acquire convictions and principles, and thus to be eventually "true to himself," rather than to be obedient to an authority. For the period we are dealing with here, that of the Bible, and for many centuries afterward, obedience and fixation are not only not identical, but they are opposites; obedience to rational authority is the path that facilitates the breaking up of incestuous fixation to preindividual archaic forces. But, in addition, *obedience to God is also the negation of submission to man.*

We find in the story of Samuel's argument with the

* Cf. for a full discussion of incestuous fixation, E. Fromm, *The Heart of Man*, Chap. V.

Hebrews, when they ask him to let them have a king (1 Sam. 8:5), that obedience to secular authority is understood as being disobedience to God: "For they have not rejected you [Samuel], but they have rejected me from being king over them," says God (1 Sam. 8:7).

The principle that man should not be the servant of man is clearly established in the Talmud in the law formulated by Rab saying that "a labourer is entitled to withdraw [from his work, that is, to strike] even in the middle of the day." Raba interprets Rab's saying: "As it is written: For to me the people of Israel are servants; they are my servants (Lev. 25:55). [This means] but not servants to servants" (Baba Kama 116b). Here the worker's right to strike without previous warning is based on the general principle of man's freedom, which is conceived as the result of man's unique obedience to God—hence not to man. The same point is made in the rabbinical comment to the law that says that a Hebrew slave's ear must be pierced if he refuses to be liberated after seven years' servitude. "R. Jochanan B. Zakkai explained to his disciples: 'The ear had heard on Mount Sinai "for unto me the children of Israel are servants" and yet this man went and acquired another master, therefore let his ear be bored through, because he observed not that which his ear had heard.' " * The same reasoning has also been used by the leaders of the Zealots, the most radical nationalistic group in the fight against Rome. As Josephus reports in his *Jewish War*, Eleazar, one of the Zealot leaders said: "We have resolved for a long time to be subject neither to the Romans nor to anybody else, except to God alone, for He

---

* Tosefta Baba Kama 7,5; quoted by A. Buechler, *op. cit.*, p. 38. The statement of R. Yohanan is also quoted by Rashi on Ex. 21:6 with regard to the piercing of the slave's ear.

is alone the true and just master of man." * The idea of
serfdom to God was, in the Jewish tradition, transformed into
the basis for the freedom of man from man. *God's authority
thus guarantees man's independence from human authority.*

There is an interesting law of the Mishnah: "If [a man's]
own lost article and his father's lost article [need attention],
his own takes precedence; his father's and his teacher's—his
teacher's takes precedence, because his father brought him
into the world, whereas his teacher, who instructed him in
wisdom, brings him to the future world; but if his father is
a sage, his father's takes precedence. If his father and his
teacher were [each] carrying a burden, he must [first] assist
his teacher to lay it down, and then assist his father. If his
father and his teacher are in captivity, he must [first]
redeem his teacher and then his father, but if his father is
a sage, he must [first] redeem his father and then his
teacher" (Baba Metzia, II, 11).

The paragraph quoted here demonstrates how the Jewish
tradition has developed from the biblical demand of obedience to father to a position where the blood relationship to
the father has become secondary to the spiritual relationship
to the teacher. (It is also interesting that in reference to the
concern for a lost article, a man's own interest takes precedence over the interest of his teacher *and* of his father.) The
spiritual authority of the teacher has superseded the natural
authority of the father, even though the biblical command
to honor one's parents has not been voided.

The goal of man's development is that of freedom and
independence. Independence means the cutting of the umbilical cord and the ability to owe one's existence to oneself
alone. But is such radical independence at all possible for

* Quoted by A. Buechler, *ibid.*, p. 36.

man? Can man face his aloneness without collapsing from terror?

Not just the child, but even man the adult is powerless. "Against *your* will you are formed and against your will you are born and against your will you live and against your will you die . . . and against your will you are destined to render an account to the King of kings, the Holy One Blessed Be He" (R. Eleazar ha-Kappar, Pirkei Avot, IV, 29). Man is aware of the risks and dangers of his existence, yet his defenses are insufficient. Eventually he succumbs to illness and old age, and dies. Those whom he loves die before him, or after him, and there is no comfort in either case. Man is uncertain; his knowledge is fragmentary. In his uncertainty he looks for absolutes that promise certainty, which he can follow, with which he can identify. Can he do without such absolutes? Is it not a question of choosing between better or worse absolutes, that is to say, between absolutes which help his development and those that hinder it? Is it not a question of choosing between God and idols?

Indeed, full independence is one of the most difficult achievements; even if man overcomes his fixation to blood and soil, to mother and clan, he holds on to other powers that give him security and certainty: his nation, his social group, his family; or his achievements, his power, his money. Or he becomes so narcissistic that he does not feel a stranger in the world because *he* is the world, there is nothing besides and outside of him.

Independence is not achieved simply by not obeying mother, father, state, and the like. Independence is not the same as disobedience. Independence is possible only if, and according to the degree to which, man actively grasps the world, is related to it, and thus becomes one with it. There is no independence and no freedom unless man arrives at the stage of complete inner activity and productivity.

The answer of the Bible and of the later Jewish tradition seems to be: indeed, man is feeble and weak, but he is an open system which can develop up to the point where he is free. He needs to be obedient to God so that he can break his fixation to the primary ties and not submit to man.

But is the concept of man's freedom carried to the ultimate consequence of his freedom *from* God? In general this is undoubtedly not the case. God, in the rabbinical literature, is conceived as being the supreme ruler and lawgiver. He is the King above all kings, and those laws for which reason can find no explanation must be followed for no other reason than that God has commanded them. Yet, while this is generally true, there are statements in the Talmudic law and later Jewish literature which are indicative of a trend that is to make man completely autonomous, even to the point where he will be free from God or, at least, where he can deal with God on terms of equality. A manifestation of the idea of man's autonomy can be found in the following Talmudic story:

On that day [in a discussion about ritual cleanliness] R. Eliezer brought forward every imaginable argument, but they did not accept them. He said to them: "If the *halakhah* agrees with me, let this carob tree prove it!" Thereupon the carob tree was torn a hundred cubits out of its place—others affirm, four hundred cubits. "No proof can be brought from a carob tree," they retorted. Again he said to them: "If the *halakhah* agrees with me, let the stream prove it!" Thereupon the stream flowed backward. "No proof can be brought from a stream of water," they rejoined. Again he urged: "If the *halakhah* agrees with me, let the walls of the schoolhouse prove it." Thereupon the walls inclined as if to fall. But R. Joshua rebuked them, saying: "When scholars are engaged in a halakhic dispute, what have you to interfere?" Hence they did not fall, in honor of R. Joshua, nor did they resume the upright position, in honor of R. Eliezer. And they are still standing thus inclined. Again R. Eliezer said to them: "If the *halakhah* agrees with me, let it be proved from Heaven!" Thereupon a heavenly voice cried out: "Why do you dispute with R. Eliezer, seeing that in all matters the *halakhah* agrees with him!" But R. Joshua arose and exclaimed: "It is not in heaven!" What did he mean by this? R. Jeremiah said: That the Torah had already been given at Mount Sinai; we pay no attention to a heavenly voice, because thou hast long since written in the Torah at Mount Sinai that after the majority must one incline.* R. Nathan met Elijah and asked him: What did the Holy One Blessed Be He, do in that hour? He laughed [with joy], he replied, and said, "My sons have defeated me, my sons have defeated me" (Baba Metzia 59b).

* R. Eliezer was later excommunicated for his failure to accept the legal decisions of the majority (not for an error in belief). A deeply human attitude, a lack of fanaticism, is shown on this occasion by R. Akiba. When the rabbis ask who should go and inform R. Eliezer: " 'I will go,' answered R. Akiba, 'lest an unsuitable person go and inform him and thus destroy the whole world' [that is, commit a great wrong by informing him tactlessly and brutally]. What did R. Akiba do? He donned black garments and wrapped himself in black [as a sign of mourning which a person under the ban had to observe]. 'Akiba,' said R. Eliezer to him, 'what has particularly happened today?' 'Master,' he replied, 'it appears to me that thy companions hold aloof from thee.' Thereupon he [R. Akiba], too, rent his garments, put off his shoes, removed [from his seat] and sat on the earth, whilst tears streamed from his eyes" (Baba Metzia 59b).

God's smile when he says "My sons have defeated me" is a paradoxical comment. The very fact that man has made himself independent and does not need God any longer, the fact of having been defeated by man is precisely what pleases God. It is in the same sense that the Talmud says: "The character of mortal man is such that when he is conquered he is unhappy, but when the Holy One is conquered, he rejoices" (Pesahim 119a). Indeed, this is a long way from the God who expelled Adam and Eve from Paradise because he was afraid they would become God themselves.

Hasidic literature is full of examples of the same spirit of independence from, and even challenge to, God. Thus, the Lizensker said: "It is a grace to God that His Zaddikim [the Hasidic masters] overrule him." *

That man can challenge God by a formal juridical procedure if God does not live up to his obligations is expressed in the following story:

A terrible famine once occurred in Ukraine and the poor could buy no bread. Ten Rabbis assembled at the home of the "Spoler Grandfather" for a session of the Rabbinical Court. The Spoler said to them:

"I have a case in judgment against the Lord. According to Rabbinical law, a master who buys a Jewish serf for a designated time (six years or up to the Jubilee year) must support not only him but also his family. Now the Lord bought us in Egypt as his serfs, since He says: 'For to Me are the sons of Israel serfs,' and the Prophet Ezekiel declared that even in Exile, Israel is the slave of God. Therefore, O Lord, I ask that Thou abide by the Law and support Thy serfs with their families."

* Quoted by L. Newman, *The Hasidic Anthology*, p. 134.

The ten judges rendered judgment in favor of the Spoler Rabbi. In a few days a large shipment of grain arrived from Siberia, and bread could be bought by the poor.*

The following story expresses the same spirit of challenge to God:

A poor man came to the Radviller Rabbi and complained of his poverty. The Radviller had no money to give him, but, in lieu of a donation, he comforted him with the words of the verse (Proverbs 3:12): "For whom the Lord loveth He correcteth."

His father, the Zlotzover Maggid, witnessed this and said to his son: "Truly this is an unworthy way to aid the indigent. The verse should be understood thus: 'For he that loveth the Lord shall argue with Him.' He should plead: 'Why shouldst Thou cause a man to put himself to shame by begging aid, when it is in Thy power, O Lord, to vouchsafe him his necessities in an honorable fashion?'" †

The idea of man's independence is expressed in the following stories:

Said the Berditschever: "We read (Isaiah 40:31): 'They that wait upon the Lord shall exchange strength.' This means that those who seek the Lord give their strength

* J. Rosenberg, *Tifereth Maharal* (Lodz, 1912); quoted by L. Newman, p. 56.

† A. Kahan, *Atereth ha-Zaddikim* (Warsaw, 1924), pp. 18–19; quoted by L. Newman, p. 57.

unto Him, and receive in return from Him new strength
to serve Him further." *

Or:

The Lubavitzer Rabbi said: "On the first day of the Festi-
val, God invites us to observe a day of rejoicing; on the second day, we invite the Lord to rejoice with us. The first day
God commanded us to observe; the second day we insti-
tuted ourselves." †

The idea that man has been created in the image of God
leads not only to the concept of man's equality with God,
or even freedom from God, it also leads to a central humanist
conviction that every man carries within himself all of
humanity.

At first glance, however, it may appear as though the
Bible and later Jewish tradition are profoundly nationalistic
in outlook, sharply separating the Hebrews from the rest of
mankind, in essence and in destiny. Is not Israel "the chosen
people," God's favorite son, superior to all other nations?
Are there not many nationalistic and xenophobic passages
in the Talmud? Have not the Jews, in their historical existence, often been nationalistic, tending to feel superior to the
Gentiles, and exhibiting a good deal of clannishness? No one
can deny this, and there is no need to bring proof of it.
In fact, it was the very essence of Pauline and later Christianity to liberate itself from all Jewish nationalism and to
found a "catholic" church, embracing all men, without
regard to nationality or race.

* I. Berger, *Esser Oroth* (Warsaw, 1913), p. 59; quoted by L.
Newman, p. 132.
 † Quoted by L. Newman, p. 176.

If we examine this nationalistic attitude, we are tempted at first to pardon it by explaining it. The earlier periods of Jewish history were those of a small tribe, fighting against other tribes and nations, and we can hardly expect to find ideas of internationalism and universalism under such circumstances. The history of the Jews after the seventh century B.C. is that of a small nation threatened in its existence by big powers trying to conquer and enslave it. First, their land is occupied by the Babylonians, and many are forced to leave their country and settle in that of the conqueror. Centuries later, Palestine is invaded by the Romans, the Temple is destroyed, many Jews are killed, made prisoners and slaves, and even the practice of their religion is forbidden under penalty of death. Later still, throughout the centuries in exile, the Jews have been persecuted, discriminated against, killed and humiliated by the Crusaders, the Spaniards, the Ukrainians, the Russians and the Poles, and, in our century, over a third of them were destroyed by the Nazis. Aside from favorable periods under Moslem rule Jews have, even under the best Christian rulers, been considered inferior and forced to live in ghettos. Is it not natural that they developed a hatred of their oppressors and a reactive nationalistic pride and clannishness to compensate for their chronic humiliations? Yet, all these circumstances only explain the existence of Jewish nationalism; they cannot condone it.

However, it is important to note that nationalistic attitudes, while *one* element in the biblical and later Jewish tradition, are balanced by the very opposite principle: that of universalism.

The idea of the unity of the human race has its first expression in the story of the creation of man. *One* man and *one* woman were created to be the forebears of the entire human race—more specifically, of the great groups into which the Bible divides mankind: the descendants of Shem, Ham, and Japhet. The second expression of the universality of the human race is found in the covenant which God makes with Noah. This covenant is concluded before the one with Abraham, the founder of the Hebrew tribe. It is a covenant with the entire human race and the animal kingdom, promising that God will never again destroy life on earth. The first challenge to God, demanding that he not violate the principle of justice, is made by Abraham in behalf of the non-Hebrew cities of Sodom and Gomorrah, not on behalf of Hebrews. The Bible commands love for the stranger (the non-Hebrew)—not only for the neighbor— and explains this command by saying: "for you were sojourners in the land of Egypt" (Deut. 10:19). Even with regard to the traditional enemy, the Edomites, it is said: "You shall not abhor an Edomite, for he is your brother" (Deut. 23:7).

The highest point of universalism is reached in the prophetic literature. While in some prophetic speeches the idea of the superiority of the Hebrews, as teachers and spiritual examples, over the Gentiles is upheld, we find other statements in which the role of the children of Israel as God's favorites is abandoned.

The idea of the unity of the human race finds its continuation in the Pharisaic literature, particularly in the Talmud. I have already mentioned the concept of the Noachites and that of the "pious among the nations."

Of the many other Talmudic statements which express the spirit of universalism and humanism a few follow:

"It has been taught: R. Meir used to say: the dust of the first man was gathered from all parts of the earth. R. Oshaiah said in Rab's name: Adam's trunk came from Babylon, his head from Israel, his limbs from other lands, and his private parts, according to R. Acha, from Akra di Agma" (Sanhedrin 38a,b). Even though in R. Oshaiah's statement the land of Israel is described as having given the material for man's head and thus his most dignified part, this qualification does not alter the essence of the first and more general statement, that man's body was made from the dust of all parts of the earth, that is, that Adam represents all of humanity.

A similar idea is expressed in a passage of the Mishnah dealing with the law that states that in a capital case, the witnesses against the accused are subjected to a procedure of intimidation ("one intimidates them") lest they bear false witness against the accused. In this procedure the witnesses are told what it means if because of their testimony a man is executed. "For this reason," they are told, "was man created alone, to teach thee that whosoever destroys a single soul of Israel * Scripture imputes guilt to him as if he had destroyed a complete world. And he who saves a single soul is considered as if he had saved a complete world . . ." (Sanhedrin IV, 5)

Another Talmudic source manifests the same spirit: "In that hour [when the Egyptians perished in the Red Sea] the ministering angels wished to utter the song [of praise]

* "Of Israel" is absent in some texts. It would seem, indeed, illogical if reference were made here to a soul of Israel, that this should be followed by a reference to destroying a complete world. If "of Israel" were part of the original text, it should continue "as if he had destroyed all of *Israel.*" Furthermore, the whole passage refers to the creation of Adam, not that of Israel, hence what is meant quite clearly is that one man (like Adam) represents all of mankind.

before the Holy One Blessed Be He, but he rebuked them saying: My handiwork [the Egyptians] is drowning in the sea; would you utter song before me?" (Sanhedrin 39b) *

In the periods of persecution of the Jews by the Romans and Christians, the nationalistic and xenophobic spirit often prevailed over the universalistic one. Yet, as long as the prophetic teachings remained alive, the idea of the unity of mankind could not be forgotten. We find manifestations of this spirit whenever the Jews had the opportunity to leave the narrow confines of their ghetto existence. Not only did they blend their own tradition with that of the leading humanist thinkers of the outside world, but when the political and social barriers broke in the nineteenth century, Jewish thinkers were among the most radical representatives of internationalism and of the idea of humanism. It seems that after two thousand years the universalism and humanism of the prophets blossomed in the figures of thousands of Jewish philosophers, socialists, and internationalists, many of whom had no personal connection with Judaism.

* It is interesting that from this tradition a liturgical practice developed which has lasted to this day. On each holy day, it is part of the service to recite a number of the joyous Hallelujah Psalms. On the seventh day of Passover when, according to tradition, the Egyptians drowned, only half of the Hallelujah Psalms are recited, following the spirit of God's rebuke to the angels who rejoiced when God's creatures died.

iv *The Concept of*
HISTORY

1   *On the Possibility of Revolution*

With Adam's "fall," human history began. The original, preindividualist harmony between man and nature, and between man and woman, was replaced by conflict and struggle. Man suffers from this loss of oneness. He is alone and separated from his fellow man, and from nature. His most passionate striving is to return to the world of union which was his home before he "disobeyed." His desire is to give up reason, self-awareness, choice, responsibility, and to return to the womb, to Mother Earth, to the darkness where the light of conscience and knowledge does not yet shine. He wants to escape from his newly gained freedom and to lose the very awareness which makes him human.

But he cannot go back. The acts of disobedience, the knowledge of good and evil, self-awareness, are irreversible. There is no way to turn back. "Therefore the Lord God sent him forth from the garden of Eden, to till the ground from which he was taken. He drove out the man; and at the east of the garden of Eden he placed the cherubim, and a flaming sword which turned every way, to guard the way to the tree of life" (Gen. 3:23–24).

Man is beset by the existential dichotomy of being within nature and yet transcending it by the fact of having self-awareness and choice; he can solve this dichotomy only by going forward. Man has to experience himself as a stranger in the world, estranged from himself and from nature, in order to be able to become one again with himself, with his fellow man, and with nature, on a higher level. He has to experience the split between himself as subject and the world as object as the condition for overcoming this very split.

Man creates himself in the historical process which began with his first act of freedom—the freedom to disobey—to say "no." This "corruption" lies in the very nature of human existence. Only by going through the process of alienation can man overcome it and achieve a new harmony. This new harmony, the new oneness with man and nature, is called in the prophetic and rabbinic literature "the end of the days," or "the messianic time." It is not a state predetermined by God or the stars; it will not happen except through man's own effort. The messianic time is the historical answer to the existence of man. He can destroy himself or advance toward the realization of the new harmony. Messianism is not accidental to man's existence but the inherent, logical answer to it—the alternative to man's self-destruction.

Just as the beginning of human history is characterized by separation from home (Paradise), so the beginning of Hebrew history is characterized by leaving home. "Now the Lord said to Abraham, 'Go forth from your country and your kindred and your father's house to the land that I will show you. And I will make of you a great nation, and I will bless you, and make your name great, so that you will be a blessing. I will bless those who bless you, and him who curses you I will curse; and by you all the families of the earth will bless themselves' " (Gen. 12:1–3).

As was said in the previous chapter, the condition for human evolution is the cutting of the primary ties that bind man to his land, to his kindred, and to his father and mother. Freedom is based on the achievement of liberating oneself from the primary ties that give security, yet cripple man. In the history of Abraham, the command to leave his country precedes the promise God makes him. But, as so often in biblical style, the first sentence does not simply precede the second in time, but constitutes a condition. We might trans-late it thus: "If you get out of your country, then I will make of you . . . " (It must be noted here that the *leit motiv* of prophetic universalism appears at this moment of the con-stitution of the Hebrew tribe: through Abraham "all the families of the earth shall be blessed.") *

* There is a peculiar parallel to God's ordering Abraham to leave his father's house, and that is God's order to sacrifice Isaac. This command is interpreted as implying a test of Abraham's obedience, or an attempt to show, though indirectly, that God does not approve of the heathen ritual of child sacrifice. While these interpretations are probably correct, the text suggests still another: namely, the command to cut the ties of blood to the son. This tentative suggestion is based

The next and central event in Jewish history, after the wanderings back and forth between Egypt and Canaan,* is the story of the liberation of the Hebrews from the Egyptians. This liberation is primarily not a national but a social revolution; the Hebrews are not freed because their life as a *national* minority is intolerable but because they are enslaved by their Egyptian masters.

The Hebrews brought to Egypt by Joseph had prospered and multiplied. The Egyptians considered them a danger to the country. "Therefore they set taskmasters over them to afflict them with heavy burdens; and they built for Pharaoh store cities, Pithom and Raamses. But the more they were oppressed, the more they multiplied and the more they spread abroad. And the Egyptians were in dread of the people of Israel. So they made the people of Israel serve with rigor, and made their lives bitter with hard service, in mortar and brick, and in all kinds of work in the field; in all their work they made them serve with rigor" (Ex. 1:11–14). The oppression became still more cruel when Pharaoh ordered

---

on the formulation of the command. While in the first instance he is told to leave "your country, your kindred and your father's house," and to go to a land which God will show him, he is now told: "Take your son, your only son Isaac, whom you love, *and go to the land of* Moriah, and offer him there as a burnt offering upon one of the mountains of *which I shall tell you*" (Gen. 22:2–3). The italicized words parallel the former command. The command to sacrifice Isaac, then, would mean man must be completely free from all ties of blood—not only with father and mother, but also with his most beloved son. But "free" does not mean that man does not love his family; it means that he is not "tied" in the sense of incestuous fixation discussed in the previous chapter.

* It is interesting that Abraham sends a servant to his homeland to bring a wife to his son Isaac, but explicitly forbids Isaac to return to his homeland.

the newborn sons of all Hebrews to be killed and only
daughters to live.

At this point of the biblical story Moses is introduced. The
son of a man and a woman from the House of Levi, he was,
according to the biblical story, hidden by the banks of the
river; he was found there by Pharaoh's daughter and educated at the Pharaoh's palace.*

The text shows us the development of Moses, the liberator.
Educated as an Egyptian prince, he is aware of his Hebrew
ancestry. When he sees an Egyptian smiting a Hebrew, one
of his brothers, he is so infuriated that he slays the Egyptian.
The Pharaoh hears of this, and Moses is forced to flee. With
this impulsive act of identification with his brothers, Moses
breaks the tie with the Egyptian court and makes himself an
outcast. He could not return except as a revolutionary leader.

During his flight he comes to the home of a Midianite
priest, marries his daughter, and has a son with her whom he
calls Gershom, meaning literally "a stranger there," or as the
text says more explicitly, "I have been a sojourner in a
foreign land" (Ex. 2:22).† Again we see the *leit motiv:*
Moses must leave Egypt, the land of his birth, before he is
ready to accept God's revelation and his mission to become
the liberator. At this point the story of the Hebrew revolution begins.

* The question of the historical Moses, especially the point treated
by Freud, that the story tends to show by implication that he was
really an Egyptian, does not interest us here as we are not dealing with
the historicity of the biblical text.

† It is interesting to note that Moses marries a Gentile woman and
that King David, according to the tradition in the Book of Ruth, is
to be the descendant of a mixed marriage between a Jewish man,
Boaz, and a Moabite woman, Ruth. The universalism that finds its
full expression in the prophetic literature finds expression here too.

With it are posed some crucial historical-psychological questions. How can slaves change so that they feel the wish for freedom? As long as they are slaves they do not know freedom, and when they are free they need no revolution. Is revolution at all possible? Is the transition from serfdom to freedom possible? Furthermore, as far as the biblical concept of history is concerned, what role does God play in the process of liberation? Does he change man's heart? Does he liberate him by an act of grace? And if this does not happen, how can man do it all by himself?

Indeed, historical change and revolution seem like a logical paradox; the enslaved man has no concept of freedom —yet he cannot become free unless he has a concept of freedom. The biblical story gives an answer to this paradox. *The beginning of liberation lies in man's capacity to suffer,* and he suffers if he is oppressed, physically and spiritually. The suffering moves him to act against his oppressors, to seek the end of the oppression, although he cannot yet seek a freedom of which he knows nothing. If man has lost the capacity to suffer, he has also lost the capacity for change. In the first step of revolution, however, he develops new powers which he could not have had while he lived as a slave, and these new powers eventually make it possible for him to achieve freedom. In the process of liberation, however, he is in danger of falling back into the old pattern of slavery.

Does God make it possible for man to become free by changing his heart? Does God intervene in the historical process? No. Man is left to himself and makes his own history; God helps, but never by changing man's nature, by doing what only man can do for himself. To put it in my own nontheistic language: man is left to himself, and nobody can do for him what he is unable to do for and by himself.

The story of the liberation from Egypt, if examined in detail, demonstrates the principles just mentioned. It begins with the sentence: "In the course of those many days the king of Egypt died. And the people of Israel groaned under their bondage, and cried out for help, and their cry under bondage came up to God. And God heard their groaning, and God remembered his covenant with Abraham, with Isaac, and with Jacob. And God saw the people of Israel, and God knew their condition" (Ex. 2:23–25). The text does not say that the children of Israel cried or prayed *to* God, but that God heard their groaning by reason of their bondage and he "understood." The cry that emerged, without direction, finds its way to God, because God "understands" suffering. The Hebrew word *va-yeda* * is correctly translated as "he knew" or "he understood." As Nahmanides pointed out in his commentary: "Although the children of Israel were not deserving of release, their cry stirred God's mercy toward them." The essential point here is that the cry is *not* directed toward God, but God understands the suffering and hence decides to help.†

The next step is God's revelation to Moses as a precondition of his mission as the liberator of the children of Israel. God appears in a bush, and "the bush was burning, yet it was not consumed" (Ex. 3:2). The bush symbolizes the paradox of all spiritual existence, that in contrast to material existence its energy does not diminish while it is being used. God reveals himself to Moses not as a God of nature but as a God of history, as the God of Abraham, the God of Isaac,

* From the verb *yada*, which is often used in the sense of to know penetratingly, or profoundly. Thus it is used of God's knowledge of man and man's knowledge of man. This meaning of the word also explains why it can be used for carnal knowledge (Gen. 4:1).

† One cannot help being reminded of the prophetic sentence: "I shall be found by those who seek me not, says the Lord."

and the God of Jacob. In his revelation he repeats, in effect, the sentences which we have already discussed. He says, "I have seen the affliction of my people who are in Egypt, and have heard their cry because of their taskmasters; I know * their sufferings, and I have come down to deliver them out of the hand of the Egyptians, and to bring them up out of that land to a good and broad land, a land flowing with milk and honey" (Ex. 3:7–8). Again the text makes clear that the Hebrews have not cried to God, but because of their taskmasters, that is, their suffering, he heard them. It requires God's knowledge, his thorough understanding, to hear the cry which was never sent up to him. And again for the third time, the same idea is repeated, "And now, behold, the cry of the people of Israel has come to me, and I have seen the oppression with which the Egyptians oppress them" (Ex. 3:9). God says here that he has convinced himself of the oppression and that it and the suffering it causes are sufficient to warrant his aid. Now God conveys to Moses the direct demand, "Go, I will send you to Pharaoh that you may bring forth my people, the sons of Israel, out of Egypt."

Moses' reaction to this command is one of shock and refusal. He, like many of the later Hebrew prophets, does not want to be a prophet. (And, we might add, anyone who wants to be a prophet is not one.) † Moses' first

* Here the perfect of the word "to know" is used (*yadati*), meaning "I know completely," "I understand fully."

† The reasons for this are not difficult to see. A prophet must talk entirely out of inner need to tell his vision, and only then can his vision and voice be trusted. If, however, he is motivated by the narcissistic wish to be a leader or a savior, the validity of his message and the integrity of his voice are questionable. The absence of narcissistic motivation is one of the chief criteria for the true prophet in the past as well as now, and there is, perhaps, no other reason for their scarcity than this psychological requirement.

argument against this command is to say, "Who am I that
I should go up to Pharaoh, and bring the sons of Israel
out of Egypt?" (Ex. 3:11) These are not the words of a
man filled with the pride of being chosen for a mission,
but those of a man free of narcissism, who, in spite of his
extraordinary talents and genius, is aware of his inadequacy
for the task he is supposed to accomplish. After God has
brushed away his first plea, Moses makes a second objection:
"If I come to the people of Israel and say to them, 'The
God of your fathers has sent me to you,' and they
ask me, 'What is his name?' what shall I say to them?"
(Ex. 3:13)

Moses raises here a crucial question which touches upon
the paradox of revolution. How can the mind of a people
be appealed to when they are not ready? More specifically,
how can people be addressed in the name of the God of
history, that is, of man's self-activity, when they are accustomed to the worship of idols, idols that are *things*
which can and must have a name? God's answer is the first
of various concessions he makes to the unpreparedness of
the people. Even though he has no name, he mentions a
name to Moses, one he can use to make himself understood
to the Hebrews. The answer, as I have indicated before,
freely translated means "My name is Nameless." * It is quite
clear here that the name "nameless" is only a name given

---

* It is interesting that the commentator Obadiah ben Jacob Sforno,
Italy (1475–1550), interprets the words that are usually translated
"I am that I am" as pointing to God's determination to remove all
cruelty and bondage that would destroy human existence. In other
words, for him the essence of God is to preserve freedom and thus
life. His commentary is an example of the spirit of Renaissance
humanism, quite different from the medieval spirit we find in Rashi's
commentary.

for the moment, that in fact God has no name, being only the God of history, the God of action.*

But Moses is still not satisfied. He makes another objection, namely, that the Hebrews will not believe him and that they will say: "The Lord did not appear to you." Again God makes a concession to the understanding of the people. He teaches Moses some magic by which he can transform his staff into a serpent and by which he can make his hand leprous and then healthy again. And if they do not believe the two examples of Moses' magic, the third one will convince them: he transforms water into blood. Moses is still not willing and says: "Oh, my Lord, I am not eloquent, either heretofore or since thou hast spoken to thy servant; but I am slow of speech and of tongue" (Ex. 4:10). God's answer is that since he has created man he can also give Moses the power to speak.

At this point Moses has exhausted all his arguments and in desperation says, "Oh, my Lord, send, I pray, some other person" (Ex. 4:13). God's patience seems to be exhausted, too, and he angrily points out that Aaron, Moses' brother, is a good speaker: "And you shall speak to him and put the words in his mouth; and I will be with your mouth and with his mouth, and will teach you what you shall do. He shall speak for you to the people; and he shall be a mouth for you, and you shall be to him as God" (Ex. 4:15–16). Priesthood is thus created. Like God's name, so the function of the priest is a concession to the ignorance

* An interesting Hasidic comment on this passage may be mentioned. It is asked why God does not say, "I am the God of Abraham, Isaac, and Jacob," but rather, "I am the God of Abraham, the God of Isaac, the God of Jacob." The answer is that this formulation indicates that no two people have the same God, that God is always an individual experience of each man.

of the people; the prophet Moses is the man of insight
and knowledge; the priest Aaron is the man who translates
the insight into the language which the people can understand. The whole ambiguity of the prophet and of the
priest is already indicated here. The prophet may not be
able to reach the understanding of the people; the priest
may speak in the name of the prophet, and yet falsify his
message.

Moses returns for a short while to his wife and father-in-
law in Midian and meets his brother Aaron in the wilderness. They both return to Egypt, speak to the Hebrews the
words God had told Moses, and perform different miracles
to prove their legitimacy. Then, and only then, "the people
believed; and when they heard that the Lord had visited
the people of Israel and that he had seen their affliction,
they bowed and worshiped" (Ex. 4:31). The reaction of
the people is that of idol worshipers; as I pointed out
before, submission, as expressed here in bowing low, is the
essence of idol worship.

After Moses and Aaron have persuaded the Hebrews, they
go to Pharaoh with their demand. They phrase it in terms
understandable to Pharaoh: "Thus says the Lord, the God of
Israel, 'Let my people go, that they may hold a feast to me
in the wilderness'" (Ex. 5:1). The language is that of
an idolatrous tradition. God is introduced as the national
God of Israel, and the purpose is to hold a feast to him.
Pharaoh declares that he knows nothing of this God, and
Aaron and Moses plead with him to grant their demand,
since otherwise God may "fall upon us with pestilence or
with the sword" (Ex. 5:3). The possibility that this God
is powerful, a God capable of doing great damage, is missed
by Pharaoh. He orders the burden of work to be increased,

and he adds "for they are idle; therefore they cry" (Ex. 5:8).
Pharaoh does what thousands of Pharaohs have done
before and after him. He cannot understand the wish for
freedom and explains it as a wish for idleness; furthermore,
he believes that when man is completely burdened with
work, he will forget his dreams of freedom which, to the
Pharaoh, are nothing anyway but lying words. When the
Hebrews have difficulty in fulfilling their quota of work,
the Pharaoh again says, "You are idle, you are idle; therefore you say, 'Let us go and sacrifice to the Lord' " (Ex.
5:17).

At this point the Hebrews begin to be afraid of freedom.
They blame Moses and Aaron for the increased difficulties
resulting from their first demands for freedom, and they
say to them, "The Lord look upon you and judge, because
you have made us offensive in the sight of Pharaoh and his
servants, and have put a sword in their hand to kill us"
(Ex. 5:21). The reaction of the Hebrews has occurred as
many times in history as the reaction of the Pharaoh. They
complain that their masters do not like them any longer;
they are afraid not only of hard work, or even death, but
also of losing favor, little as it was, with those who exploit
them.

Moses seems to lose his courage. He complains to God and
says: "O Lord, why hast thou done evil to this people? Why
didst thou ever send me? For since I came to Pharaoh to
speak in thy name, he has done evil to this people, and
thou hast not delivered thy people at all" (Ex. 5:22–23).

With this desperate reproach to God, the first act of the
drama has ended. Pharaoh has neither ceded to, or even
understood, the message, nor have the people continued in
their wish for freedom when the first difficulties arose.

Moses, the leader, does not see that there is any hope for the success of the revolution. At this point it seems to God that the time for an approach of reason and without force has passed. From now on force will be used, which will eventually compel Pharaoh to give in and make it possible for the Hebrews to escape from the land of slavery. Yet, as we shall see, force never convinced Pharaoh, and it never convinced the Hebrews, who regress to fear of freedom and to idol worship whenever they encounter difficulties or when the charismatic figure of the leader is not present.

The next act opens with God's command to Moses to speak again to the children of Israel:

> "I am the Lord, and I will bring you out from under the burdens of the Egyptians, and I will deliver you from their bondage, and I will redeem you with an outstretched arm and with great acts of judgment, and I will take you for my people, and I will be your God; and you shall know that I am the Lord your God, who has brought you out from under the burdens of the Egyptians. And I will bring you into the land which I swore to give to Abraham, to Isaac, and to Jacob; I will give it to you for a possession. I am the Lord." Moses spoke thus to the people of Israel; but they did not listen to Moses, because of their broken spirit and their cruel bondage.
>
> Exodus 6:6–9

Again, the language used to the children of Israel is different from that used for Pharaoh. Here the message is that they will be delivered from their bondage and that they will be aware of God as the deliverer. But again the Hebrews are deaf to the message, partly because their spirit was broken, partly because the work was so hard that they had no energy left even to suffer. We touch upon a phenomenon here which has often been repeated in history. There is a degree of suffering that deprives men even of their wish to end it. Moses also has lost his faith; when told to go to Pharaoh to demand the liberation of the Hebrews, he answers, "Behold, the people of Israel have not listened to me; how then shall Pharaoh listen to me, who am a man of uncircumcised lips?" (Ex. 6:12)

In the following chapter God confirms his command to Moses to go and see Pharaoh. He is to say to him that he should let the children of Israel go out of the land. The pretense is no longer used here that they should go only three days' journey into the desert to "celebrate." The demand is full and unconditional.

The passage which now follows is one of the most puzzling in the story. God says, "But I will harden Pharaoh's heart, and though I multiply my signs and wonders in the land of Egypt, Pharaoh will not listen to you; then I will lay my hand upon Egypt and bring forth my hosts, my people the sons of Israel out of the land of Egypt by great acts of judgment. And the Egyptians shall know that I am the Lord, when I stretch forth my hand upon Egypt and bring out the people of Israel from among them" (Ex. 7:3–6). What does God mean by saying "I will harden Pharaoh's heart"? Is this the word of a vengeful and deceitful Lord who plays a double game with Pharaoh, letting Moses ask him to let the Hebrews go and at the same time determining him not to yield? I believe this is unlikely, because the picture of God it implies is too far from even the most anthropomorphic descriptions of God we find in the Bible. It seems to me that the statement "I will harden Pharaoh's heart" is to be understood in terms of the belief that all *necessary* events are events not only predicted, but caused by God. Any act that will necessarily happen is God's will. Hence, when God says that he will harden Pharaoh's heart, he is announcing that Pharaoh's heart will unavoidably harden. And indeed, the biblical text that follows seems to confirm this, because it says many times that "Pharaoh hardened his heart." In other words, "I will harden Pharaoh's heart" and "Pharaoh hardens his heart" mean the same.

What the biblical text stresses here is one of the most fundamental laws of human behavior. Every evil act tends to harden man's heart, that is, to deaden it. Every good act tends to soften it, to make it more alive. The more man's heart hardens, the less freedom does he have to change; the more is he determined already by previous action. But there comes a point of no return, when man's heart has become so hardened and so deadened that he has lost the possibility of freedom, when he is forced to go on and on until the unavoidable end which is, in the last analysis, his own physical or spiritual destruction.*

* Cf. a detailed analysis of the problem of the hardening of the heart and that of human freedom in *The Heart of Man*, Chap. VI.

The Jewish commentators of the Bible have, of course, had their own difficulties with this sentence. Abraham ibn Ezra (born 1090 in Spain) raises the question that if God hardened Pharaoh's heart, how could Pharaoh justly be condemned for his refusal? He answers that God has endowed every man with superior wisdom and intelligence to enable him to rise above fate. But Pharaoh failed to make the attempt. But Abraham ibn Ezra assumes that man always has the freedom to rise above fate, even though fate is described here in terms of God's intention, that is, the law of cause and effect. Rashi comments in a more traditional way: God wanted Pharaoh to suffer as a punishment that would cleanse him. Nahmanides, on the contrary, expresses a view essentially like the one we have presented. He says the Pharaoh had already forfeited the chance of repentance by the wrongs he had perpetrated on Israel. What Nahmanides means here is clearly that Pharaoh had no longer the chance to "return" and that this is what the sentence about the hardening of the heart means

The new strategy toward Pharaoh does not begin with force but with the use of miracles; however, miracles are, after all, only another kind of force, one that is directed toward the mind rather than to the body. Aaron transforms his rod into a serpent. But the magicians of Egypt "did the same by their secret arts" (Ex. 7:11). Moses is told by God to perform a second miracle; he will turn the water in the river into blood; all the fish will die and the Egyptians shall loathe to drink the water from the river. But again the Egyptian magicians duplicate the miracle; Pharaoh is not impressed, and his "heart remained hardened" (Ex. 7:22). Moses and Aaron perform a third miracle: they cover the land with frogs. The Egyptian magicians can do this also; yet this miracle, while not impressive in itself, does severe damage to the whole of Egypt, and Pharaoh begins to yield. At a determined time the frogs are called back by Moses: "But when Pharaoh saw that there was a respite, he hardened his heart, and would not listen to them; as the Lord had said" (Ex. 8:15). Then God orders Moses and Aaron to bring gnats upon all of Egypt. At this point the secret arts of Moses and Aaron begin to surpass those of the Egyptian magicians. They try, but they cannot produce gnats; beaten at their own game they tell Pharaoh: " 'This is the finger of God.' But Pharaoh's heart was hardened, and he would not listen to them" (Ex. 8:19). As a next step God sends swarms of flies over all Egypt. The Egyptian magicians try but do not succeed in imitating this secret art. Pharaoh is frightened enough to promise again that he will let the Hebrews go into the desert to sacrifice to their God, but when the flies are called off "Pharaoh hardened his heart this time also, and did not let the people go" (Ex. 8:32).

Before Moses announces the next act of retaliation he introduces his demands in a new form; he asks Pharaoh to "Let my people go, that they may serve me [the Lord]" (Ex. 9:1). Next, all Egyptian cattle are killed by a plague, while the cattle of the Hebrews are not touched. "But the heart of Pharaoh was hardened." A plague of boils, breaking forth on man and beast throughout Egypt, follows. Even the magicians could not stand before Moses because of the boils. But again Pharaoh refuses to yield. Then comes another plague, destructive hail. "But when Pharaoh saw that the rain and the hail and the thunder had ceased, he sinned yet again, and hardened his heart, he and his servants. So the heart of Pharaoh was hardened, and he did not let the people of Israel go; as the Lord had spoken through Moses" (Ex. 9:34–35).

After that Moses and Aaron threaten to send locusts all over Egypt. At this point, for the first time, Pharaoh's own subjects begin to rebel. They say, "How long shall this man be a snare to us? Let the men go, that they may serve the Lord their God; do you not yet understand that Egypt is ruined?" (Ex. 10:7) Pharaoh tries to compromise. He will permit the grown men to go, but no one else. After this the locusts are brought over Egypt, and for the first time Pharaoh acknowledges his action to be wrong, saying: "I have sinned against the Lord your God, and against you. Now therefore, forgive my sin, I pray you, only this once, and entreat the Lord your God only to remove this death from me" (Ex. 10:16–17). But even in spite of this apparent repentance, when the locusts had gone "the Lord hardened Pharaoh's heart, and he did not let the children of Israel go" (Ex. 10:20).

After this, darkness descends over all Egypt, while the

children of Israel have light in their dwellings. Pharaoh is impressed, but tries to compromise again. He is willing to permit everyone to leave, but he wants the flocks and the herds to stay. Moses refuses, and Pharaoh's heart hardens again. He throws Moses out and says, "Get away from me; take heed to yourself; never see my face again; for in the day you see my face you shall die" (Ex. 10:28). And Moses says, "As you say! I will not see your face again" (Ex. 10:29). This is, indeed, the last step before the end. God threatens through Moses that he will kill all the first-born in Egypt, including the first-born son of the Pharaoh, but again Pharaoh's heart hardens. In one of the first commands found in the Bible Moses orders every man to slaughter a lamb, to put its blood on the two doorposts of the house and "They shall eat the flesh that night, roasted; with unleavened bread" (Ex. 12:8). "In this manner you shall eat it: your loins girded, your sandals on your feet, and your staff in your hand; and you shall eat it in haste. It is the Lord's passover" (Ex. 12:11). A common meal is ordered at the outset of the revolution. But a meal in haste. He who wants to be free must be prepared to march and to eat on the march, as it were. When the Hebrews have done all this, all the first-born of the Egyptians and of their cattle are killed. Now Pharaoh seems to admit his defeat: "And he summoned Moses and Aaron by night, and said, 'Rise up, go forth from among my people, both you and the people of Israel; and go, serve the Lord, as you have said. Take your flocks and your herds, as you have said, and be gone; and bless me also!" (Ex. 12:31–32)

The Hebrews, loaded with "gifts" from the desperate Egyptians, march out, "about six hundred thousand men on foot, besides women and children" (Ex. 12:37). The Passover service, in commemoration of the liberation, is commanded to be observed for all the future. Furthermore, as a memorial and perhaps as a reconciliation with God, it is ordered that "all the firstlings of your cattle that are males shall be the Lord's" (Ex. 13:12).

After the children of Israel left Egypt, the Lord "went before them by day in a pillar of cloud to lead them along the way, and by night in a pillar of fire" (Ex. 13:21). But, for the last time, Pharaoh cannot accept his loss:

> When the king of Egypt was told that the people had fled, the mind of Pharaoh and his servants was changed toward the people, and they said, "What is this we have done, that we have let Israel go from serving us?" So he made ready his chariot and took his army with him. . . . And the Lord hardened the heart of Pharaoh king of Egypt and he pursued the people of Israel. . . . When Pharaoh drew near, the people of Israel lifted up their eyes, and behold, the Egyptians were marching after them; and they were in great fear. And the people of Israel cried out to the Lord; and they said to Moses, "Is it because there are no graves in Egypt that you have taken us away to die in the wilderness? What have you done to us, in bringing us out of Egypt? Is not this what we said to you in Egypt, 'Let us alone and let us serve the Egyptians'? For it would have been better for us to serve the Egyptians than to die in the wilderness."
>
> Exodus 14:5–12

The Hebrews have changed as little as Pharaoh. They leave Egypt under the protection of force and lose heart when superior forces seem to be looming. Pharaoh yields before the threat of force and takes heart when the force seems to be decreasing. At last the drama has reached its conclusion. God lets Moses make use for the last time of the "secret arts," and "Moses stretched out his hand over the sea; and the Lord drove the sea back by a strong east wind all night, and made the sea dry land, and the waters were divided. And the people of Israel went into the midst of the sea on dry ground, the waters being a wall to them on their right hand and on their left. The Egyptians pursued, and went in after them into the midst of the sea, all Pharaoh's horses, his chariots, and his horsemen" (Ex. 14:21-23). When the Egyptians were in the midst of the sea "the waters returned and covered the chariots and the horsemen and all the hosts of Pharaoh that had followed them into the sea." The Hebrews walked across and were saved. "And Israel saw the great work which the Lord did against the Egyptians, and the people feared the Lord; and they believed in the Lord and in his servant Moses" (Ex. 14:28-31).

The last sentence of this act of the drama implies again that the heart of the Hebrews had not changed. Seeing the Egyptian army dead, they "feared the Lord" (just as Pharaoh had feared him when he saw the deeds of destruction), and because they feared him they believed in him, as many men before and after them have believed in God only when they were afraid.

If we try to sum up the analysis of the essential features of this story, several things become clear. The possibility of liberation exists only because people suffer and, in biblical language, because God "understands" the suffering and hence tries to relieve it. Indeed, there is nothing more human than suffering, and there is nothing that unites men more than suffering. Only a minority of men throughout all of past history have had more than a glimpse of happiness during their lifetimes, but all have experienced suffering: the less sensitive only their own; those with greater sensitivity, that of many around them. But man's suffering does not mean that he knows where to go and what to do. It creates only the wish that the suffering may stop. And this wish is the first and the necessary impulse for liberation. In the biblical story God "understands" the suffering. He sends his messenger to urge and coax the Hebrews and their masters to stop being locked up together as masters and prisoners. But neither of them can understand the language of freedom or of reason; they understand, so the report tells us, only the language of force. But this language does not lead very far. It is no lesson; it merely causes the oppressed to hope and the oppressor to yield, when force is successful.

Anyone who reads the story attentively will recognize that the miracles Moses and Aaron perform on behalf of God are not miracles intended to change man's heart. In the first place they are from the very beginning meant only to impress both the Hebrews and the Egyptians. They are in their nature no different from what the Egyptian magicians are able to do, except that eventually the Hebrews' secret weapons prove to be a little more effective. The irony of the story is that the all-powerful God chose miracles which repeat, or only slightly improve on, Egyptian magic.

Indeed, perhaps never in human history has it been possible to understand this part of the biblical story as well as today. Two powerful blocs of mankind are attempting to find a solution to the threat of weapons—weapons compared to which the ten plagues appear harmless. Until now both sides have shown better sense than did Pharaoh; they have yielded before arriving at the use of nuclear force (although this has not prevented them from using force against those who had no such weapons at their disposal). But they have not given up the principle of preferring to see the world destroyed, rather than not to prevail against the other. They believe that the threat of force will guarantee "freedom" or "communism"—as the case may be. They do not see that this course only hardens man's heart more and more, until he arrives at the point where he ceases to care; at this point he will act as did Pharaoh, and perish as did the Egyptians.

The second act of the drama of the Hebrew revolution is completed, and it concludes with a beautiful poem sung by Moses and the children of Israel, ending with the words of hope: "The Lord will reign for ever and ever" (Ex. 15:18). This was accompanied by Miriam the prophetess, who went forth with all the women with timbrels and with dances.

The third act is the wandering of the Hebrews in the wilderness. They had suffered in Egypt; they had been brought out from slavery, but where had they been brought? Into the wilderness, where they often suffered hunger and thirst. They are dissatisfied and they grumble, allegedly because they do not have enough to eat. But can one overlook the fact that they were afraid of more than hunger? They were afraid also of freedom. They were afraid because they did not have the well-regulated and set existence under which they had lived in Egypt—even though it was the life of slaves—because they had no overseer and no king and no idols before whom they could bow down. They were afraid because they were a people who had nothing but a prophet as a leader, provisional tents for dwellings, and no set task except that of marching forward toward an unknown goal.

Their security in Egypt as slaves appears to them far

preferable to the insecurity of freedom. They say, "Would that we had died by the hand of the Lord in the land of Egypt, when we sat by the fleshpots and ate bread to the full; for you have brought us out into this wilderness to kill this whole assembly with hunger" (Ex. 16:3). It seems that God understands that slaves, even after they have freed themselves, remain slaves at heart, and therefore there is no reason to be angry. He provides them with bread, the manna they find every morning. There are two commands connected with the gathering of the manna, and both are very significant. One is that they must not take more than they can eat in one day (those who collect more find the excess to be full of worms on the following morning). The meaning of this command is clear: food is meant to be eaten and not to be saved; life is to be lived, not to be hoarded. Just as there are no houses in the wilderness, there is also no property. In a climate of freedom all things serve life, but life does not serve property.

The other, and still more important, command connected with the collection of the manna is that of the institution of the Sabbath day, which appears here for the first time. The people are to gather manna every day; on the sixth day they are to collect twice the daily portion (and what is left will not be spoilt on the seventh day), and "At evening you shall know that it was the Lord who brought you out of the land of Egypt" (Ex. 16:6).

When their hunger is stilled, their thirst drives them to new anger. They say: "Why did you bring us out of Egypt, to kill us and our children and our cattle with thirst?" (Ex. 17:3) At this even Moses loses his patience, or perhaps his faith, and "Moses cried to the Lord, 'What shall I do with this people? They are almost ready to stone me'" (Ex. 17:4).

Again God provides; Moses smites a rock, and water gushes out so that the people have enough to drink.

The central event in the forty years' wandering in the desert is the announcement of the Ten Commandments. A new and important concept is proclaimed: "And you shall be to me a kingdom of priests and a holy nation" (Ex. 19:6). If the whole nation is a nation of priests, then indeed, there are no longer any priests, since the whole concept of priesthood is that of a separate caste set above the nation. This concept of the "nation of priests" contains the negation of priesthood. Later on, of course, the Hebrews were to have a priesthood, and an increasingly powerful one, until the destruction of the Second Temple by the Romans; but from then on their religion would be free from priesthood, and the idea announced in the wilderness would take on new meaning. They are to be a nation of priests, that is, a holy nation without priests.*

Moses is summoned by God to go to the top of the mountain, while Aaron is to stay with the people. After forty days and forty nights Moses is given the Ten Commandments, written on two tables of stone. But he is given not only these tablets; he is also given the command to make a sanctuary that can be transported, a small temple, as it were, with all sorts of vessels and ornaments. At the center of it is to be an ark, overlaid with pure gold, and a crown of gold round about it. Also, he is told what sacred garment Aaron and the other priests shall wear when they officiate as

* The Jews, after the destruction of the Second Temple, when the priesthood lost its function, continued to remember the lineage of *kohanim* (priests) and to give them the privilege of reciting the traditional blessing in the services; but, of course, this is only a feeble reminder of a powerful caste of priests who at one time were the center of the religious system.

priests. These ordinances for the ark, for the priests, and
for the sacrifices seem to have been given because God knew
how much the Hebrews longed for visible symbols; it was
no longer enough for them to be led by a God who had
no name, who was not represented visibly.

Indeed, after Moses, their only visible leader, had gone to
the mountain, the people came to Aaron and said to him:
"Up, make us gods, who shall go before us; as for this
Moses, the man who brought us up out of the land of Egypt,
we do not know what has become of him" (Ex. 32:1). Moses,
the leader to freedom, has become "that man." The people
felt relatively secure as long as he, the powerful leader, the
miracle worker, the feared authority, was present. Once he
is absent, even for only a few days, they are gripped again
with the fear of freedom. They long for another reassuring
symbol. They want Aaron, the priest, to make a god for
them. Not being alive, such a god can also not absent himself; being visible, no faith is required. The horde of slaves,
catapulted into freedom by a forceful leader, reassured
many times by miracles, food, and drink, cannot stand being
without a visible symbol to submit to.

Aaron tries to delay the matter by asking them to give
him their gold jewelry. But they are quite willing to sacrifice
their gold in exchange for certainty. Aaron, with a heavy
heart, to be sure, betrays his faith and his loyalty to Moses.
As many priests and politicians have done after him, he
hoped to "save" the idea by destroying it. Perhaps, also,
to preserve the unity of the people he sacrifices the truth that
alone gives meaning to unity. Aaron fashions them a golden
calf, and the Hebrews say: "These are your gods, O Israel,
who brought you up out of the land of Egypt!" (Ex. 32:4)
In spite of the "living God" who brought them out of

Egypt, the Hebrews now have returned to the worship of an idol made of gold, an idol who can neither walk before them nor after them, because it is dead.

And now God, for the first time in the history of the liberation, loses not only his patience but his hope. After all the concessions he has made to the ignorance and weakness of the people it seems futile—whether we speak in terms of God or in terms of the historical process—to expect that this revolution will ever succeed. If a relatively short absence of the leader results in making the people regress fully to idol worship then, indeed, how can one expect that they will ever become free? So God says: "I have seen this people, and behold, it is a stiff-necked people; now therefore let me alone, that my wrath may burn hot against them and I may consume them; but of you I will make a great nation" (Ex. *32*:9–10). This is the greatest temptation Moses was ever exposed to: to be made not only the leader but the founder of a new and great nation. Moses is not tempted. He reminds God of his covenant with Abraham and here, as in the case of Abraham, God yields when he is reminded of his promises. And so "the Lord repented of the evil which he thought to do to his people" (Ex. *32*:14).

When Moses came down from the mountain with the two tables with God's writing on them in his hands, he saw the calf and the people dancing around it, "and Moses' anger burned hot, and he threw the tables out of his hands and broke them at the foot of the mountain" (Ex. *32*:19). At this moment Moses is fully alive in his anger and is not even restrained by the fear of committing a sacrilege in destroying the tables on which God himself has written. He destroys the golden calf, and he has the men of his tribe, Levi, kill the worshipers of the calf. Then he asks God to forgive the people, and God renews his promise to bring them to the promised land.

God makes a new covenant with Moses and promises him that he will drive out the idolatrous tribes living in the land the Hebrews are to occupy. He forbids him to make any covenant with them, but to "tear down their altars, and break their pillars, and cut down their Asherim, for you shall worship no other god" (Ex. 34:13–14).

There are many more years during which the Hebrews wander in the desert, and many laws and ordinances are given them. Eventually the time for the end of the last act of the revolution has come, and Moses himself must die and cannot go beyond the Jordan into the promised land. He, too, is a member of a generation that grew up in idol worship and serfdom, and even though he was God's messenger, filled with the vision of a new life, he was held back by his past and could not participate in the future. The death of Moses completes the biblical answer to the question of the possibility of revolution. Revolution can succeed only in steps in time. Suffering produces rebellion; rebellion produces freedom *from* serfdom; freedom *from* may eventually lead to freedom *to* a new life without idolatry. But since there is no miraculous change of heart, each generation can take only one step. Those who have suffered and started the revolution cannot go beyond the limits their past sets for them. Only those who have not been born in slavery may succeed in achicving the promised land.

The death of Moses finds an explicit explanation in still another factor. God reproaches him with "having broken faith with him," with "not having revered him" when he brought forth the waters in the desert of Zin (Deut. 32:48–52). The prophet who even for a moment puts himself in the center shows that he is not ready to be a leader *in* freedom, but only *to* freedom. Joshua is to continue in his place.

The rest of the Old Testament is a report of the failure in this task. After having used force pitilessly to rid themselves of contamination by idolatry, the Hebrews embraced idolatry wholeheartedly, disguising it only by retaining the old sacred names. Perhaps they could not have done otherwise because of the effect of the inhuman fanaticism they employed in the conquest of Canaan. Could they become a "holy people" after ruthlessly killing men, women, and children in order to protect themselves from the danger of idolatry? If this inhumanity was necessary to preserve their faith, they were destined to fall back into idolatry in any case, and the cruelty of their warfare served no good purpose.

The first revolution had failed. While in Egypt, the Hebrews were idolaters and slaves on foreign soil; in Canaan they were idolaters on their own soil. The only difference was that they were free, politically at least. But even this freedom was to last only a short time. After a few centuries they were again subjected to the will of foreign conquerors, and they were to remain virtually without power for the next twenty-five hundred years of their history.

Does, then, the revolution end in nothing but defeat? Is the new idolatry and the ruthless nationalism in the conquered land the end of the striving for independence? Are a number of old stones in Jerusalem all that is left of a glorious attempt to build the heavenly city?

It might have been so, but it happened otherwise. The idea of the One who loves truth and justice but whose love is greater even than his justice, the idea that man must find his goal by becoming fully human, was carried on by men of vision—the prophets. Their teachings became increasingly impressive because history bore them out. Secular power, which reached its peak under Solomon, collapsed after a few centuries, never to be restored in an impressive way. History vindicated those who spoke the truth, not those who held power. After the failure of the first prophet, Moses, new prophets continued his work, deepened and clarified his ideas, and developed a concept of history which, although its seeds were contained in the earlier period, was to flower only in the prophetic literature, in the concept of the messianic time, which was to have the deepest influence on the development not only of the history of the Jews but of the whole world, first in the form of Christianity and then in secularized form, socialism, even though both Christianity and socialism in their institutionalized forms distorted the original vision.

2 Man as the Maker of His History

With the death of Moses the revolution against serfdom and idolatry had failed. Man's craving for certainty and for submission to idols had proved to be stronger than his faith in the unknowable God and his wish for freedom. But why was this failure necessary? Could God not have saved man by changing his heart through an act of grace? This question touches upon the fundamental principle of the biblical and post-biblical concept of history.

The principle I refer to is that man makes his own history and that God does not interfere by an act of grace or by coercion; he does not change the nature of man, nor his heart.

If God had so wanted, he could have changed Adam's and

Eve's hearts and prevented their "fall." If God had wanted to, he could have changed Pharaoh's heart, instead of permitting it to harden; he could have changed the Hebrews' hearts, so that they would not have worshiped the golden calf and then fallen into new idolatry after having conquered the promised land. Why did God not do so? Was he lacking in power? There is only one reason for the account as it stands: that man is free to choose his way and yet must accept the consequences of his choice.

It might seem that this principle is contradicted by the miracles God performs in Egypt. But they are not essential. They are, as I pointed out before, tactical devices designed to impress both the Egyptians and the Hebrews. They are not miracles that save man, change his heart, transform his substance, but they are the kind of help a powerful war lord would give his weak allies. They are not an act of grace God would bestow on his creatures. The Jewish tradition has felt this very keenly. The Midrash (Ex. Rabbah XXI, 10) reports that when Moses cast his staff into the Red Sea the waters did not recede. Only when the first Hebrew stepped into the sea did the miracle occur.

Maimonides has expressed the idea that God does not change man's heart:

Although in every one of the signs [related in Scripture] the natural property of some individual being is changed, the nature of man is never changed by God by way of miracle. It is in accordance with this important principle that God said, "O that there were such an heart in them, that they would fear me" (Deut. 26). It is also for this reason that He distinctly stated the commandments and prohibitions, the reward and the punishment. This prin-

ciple as regards miracles has been frequently explained
by us in our works; I do not say this because I believe
that it is difficult for God to change the nature of every
individual person; on the contrary, it is possible, and it is
in His power, according to the principles taught in
Scripture; but it has never been His will to do it, and
it never will be. If it were part of His will to change [at
His desire] the nature of any person, the mission of the
prophets and the giving of the Law would have been
altogether superfluous.*

If it is true that God leaves man free to shape his own
history, does this mean that he is a passive spectator of
man's fate, that he is not the God who reveals himself in
history? The answer to this question lies in the role and
function of the prophets, of whom Moses was the first.
God's role in history is to send his messengers, the prophets;
they have a fourfold function:

1) They announce to man that there is God, the One
who has revealed himself to them, and that man's goal is
to become fully human; and that means to become like God.

2) They show man alternatives between which he can
choose, and the consequences of these alternatives. They
often express this alternative in terms of God's rewards and
punishment, but it is always man who, by his own action,
makes the choice.

3) They dissent and protest when man takes the wrong
road. But they do not abandon the people; they are their
conscience, speaking up when everybody else is silent.

4) They do not think in terms of individual salvation

* Cf. Moses Maimonides, *The Guide for the Perplexed*, III, 32,
translated by M. Friedländer.

only, but believe that individual salvation is bound up with the salvation of society. Their concern is the establishment of a society governed by love, justice, and truth; they insist that politics must be judged by moral values, and that the function of political life is the realization of these values.

The concept of the prophet is as characteristically biblical as the concept of the messianic time. The prophet is a revealer of truth; so were Lao-tse and Buddha. But he is at the same time also a political leader, deeply concerned with political action and social justice. His realm is never a purely spiritual one; it is always of *this* world. Or rather, his spirituality is always experienced in the political and social dimensions. Because God is revealed in history, the prophet cannot help being a political leader; as long as man takes the wrong way in his political action, the prophet cannot help being a dissenter and a revolutionary.

The prophet sees reality and speaks what he sees. He sees the inseparable connection between spiritual strength and historical fate. He sees the moral reality underlying social and political reality—the consequences that will necessarily result from it. He sees the possibilities of change and the direction the people must take, and he announces what he sees. As Amos says, "The lion has roared; who will not fear? The Lord God has spoken; who can but prophesy?" (Amos 3:8)

In ancient times a prophet was called *roeh,* which means "seer," but probably since the times of Elijah, the seer was called the *navi,* meaning the "speaker," or the "spokesman." The *navi,* indeed, says something about the future. But not about a future event which will necessarily occur, a fixed event revealed to him by God or by the knowledge of the astral constellations. He sees the future because he

sees the forces operating *now* and the consequences of these
forces unless they are changed. The prophet is never a
Cassandra. His prophecies are expressed in terms of alternatives.

The prophets leave room for free will and decision.
When Jonah is sent to Nineveh, a city of sinners, he does
not like his mission; he is a man of justice, but not of
mercy; he is afraid that the result of his announcement
might be a change of heart, and hence that the prophecy of
disaster would, after all, not come true. He tries to escape
from his mission, and yet he cannot escape. Like all the
prophets, he does not want to be one, and yet he cannot
avoid it. He brings his message to Nineveh and the unwanted
result occurs. The men of Nineveh change their hearts
and are forgiven by God. "But it displeased Jonah ex-
ceedingly, and he was angry. And he prayed to the Lord
and said, 'I pray thee, Lord, is not this what I said when I
was yet in my country? That is why I made haste to flee
to Tarshish; for I knew that thou art a gracious God and
merciful, slow to anger, and abounding in steadfast love, and
repentest of evil. Therefore now, O Lord, take my life
from me, I beseech thee, for it is better for me to die than
to live' " (Jonah 4:1–4). Jonah is different from all the
other prophets, inasmuch as he is not prompted by compassion and responsibility.

The clearest example of the principle of God's non-
interference and the role of the prophet is found in the
report of God's attitude when the Hebrews ask Samuel to
give them a king.

Then all the elders of Israel gathered together and
came to Samuel at Ramah, and said to him, "Behold, you

are old and your sons do not walk in your ways; now appoint for us a king to govern us like all the nations." But the thing displeased Samuel when they said, "Give us a king to govern us." And Samuel prayed to the Lord. And the Lord said to Samuel, "Hearken to the voice of the people in all that they say to you; for they have not rejected you, but they have rejected me from being king over them. According to all the deeds which they have done to me, from the day I brought them up out of Egypt even to this day, forsaking me and serving other gods, so they are also doing to you. Now then, hearken to their voice; only, you shall solemnly warn them, and show them the ways of the king who shall reign over them."

So Samuel told all the words of the Lord to the people who were asking a king from him.

1 Samuel 8:4–9

He describes how a king will exploit them; will use the men as soldiers and the women as servants; how he will take one-tenth of all their property; how the people then "will cry out because of your king, whom you have chosen for yourselves; but the Lord will not answer you in that day" (1 Sam. 8:18).

"But the people refused to listen to the voice of Samuel; and they said, 'No! but we will have a king over us, that we also may be like all the nations, and that our king may govern us and go out before us and fight our battles.' And when Samuel had heard all the words of the people, he repeated them in the ears of the Lord. And the Lord said to Samuel, 'Hearken to their voice, and make them a king.' Samuel then said to the men of Israel, 'Go every man to his city' " (1 Sam. 8:19–22).

All that Samuel can do is to "hearken to their voice" after having protested and pointed out to them the consequences of their action. If, in spite of this, the people decide for a kingdom, it is their decision and their responsibility. To put it differently: history has its own laws, and God does not interfere with them. They are at the same time God's laws. Man, in understanding the laws of history, understands God. Political action is religious action. The spiritual leader is a political leader.*

3 The Biblical Concept of the Messianic Time †

In order to discuss the concept of the messianic time it seems necessary to summarize our discussion of the "fall."

With the expulsion from Paradise, the original unity was broken. Man acquired self-awareness and awareness of his fellow man as a stranger. This awareness split him from his fellow man and from nature, and made him a stranger in the world. Becoming a stranger, however, does not mean becoming a sinner, and, even less, being corrupted. At no point in the biblical story is there any thought of man's

---

* This Old Testament concept of God as the God of history contrasts with the seventeenth-century concept of God as the God of nature. Here man, by discovering the laws of nature, knows God, and by changing nature, participates in God's work.

† For the whole problem of messianism, I have leaned heavily on Joseph Klausner, *The Messianic Idea in Israel* (London: George Allen & Unwin, 1956); A. H. Silver, *A History of Messianic Speculation in Israel* (New York: Macmillan, 1927), republished in a Beacon Paperback Edition in 1959; Julius H. Greenstone, *The Messiah Idea in Jewish History* (Philadelphia: The Jewish Publication Society of America, 1906); and Leo Baeck, *Judaism and Christianity* (Philadelphia: The Jewish Publication Society of America, 1958), translated and an introduction by W. Kaufmann.

nature being changed or corrupted; the "fall" is not a metaphysical-individual, but a historical, event.

Christian theologians read the third chapter of Genesis as a picturesque description of man sinning by refusing to believe in the divine word. The key texts for their doctrine of original sin are in St. Paul (1 Cor. 15:21 ff., and especially Rom. 5–7). Sin is no longer looked upon as an isolated action, but rather as a state in which man has been held captive since the fall. Although Catholic teaching has been that, however wounded by the consequences of original sin, man's nature is unchanged, the dominant experience of Christians, reflecting both the strict Augustinian tradition and the exaggerated pessimism of the Reformers, has been the emphasis on essential corruption. Luther and Calvin maintained that original sin completely destroyed liberty and persisted even after baptism, and for Catholics, too, only God's act of grace, his appearing on earth as Christ, his son, and dying for the sins of man can save man. As we shall see later, the view that man's substance was *not* corrupted is emphasized again and again in the messianic-prophetic concept and later, when hope for historical salvation asserted itself, as, for instance, in Renaissance humanism or in eighteenth-century Enlightenment philosophy.* One can understand neither the philosophical and political ideas of these centuries nor the messianic idea of the prophets unless one is aware of the fact that their concept of man's first "sin" is entirely different from that of "original sin" as it was developed by the church.

Seen from the standpoint of biblical philosophy, the process of history is the process in which man develops his

* Cf. Ernst Cassirer, *The Philosophy of the Enlightenment* (Boston: Beacon Press, 1955), pp. 159 ff.

powers of reason and love, in which he becomes fully human, in which he returns to himself. He regains the harmony and innocence he had lost, and yet it is a new harmony and a new innocence. It is the harmony of a man completely aware of himself, capable of knowing right and wrong, good and evil. A man who has emerged from delusion and from half-slumber, a man who has become free, finally. In the process of history man gives birth to himself. He becomes what he potentially is, and he attains what the serpent—the symbol of wisdom and rebellion—promised, and what the patriarchal, jealous God of Adam did not wish: that man would become like God himself.

The messianic time is the next step in history, not its abolition. The messianic time is the time when man will have been fully born. When man was expelled from Paradise he lost his home; in the messianic time he will be at home again—in the world.

The messianic time is not brought about by an act of grace or by an innate drive within man toward perfection. It is brought about by the force generated by man's existential dichotomy: being part of nature and yet transcending nature; being animal and yet transcending animal nature. This dichotomy creates conflict and suffering, and man is driven to find ever new solutions to this conflict, until he has solved it by becoming fully human and achieving at-onement.

There is a dialectic relationship between Paradise and the messianic time. Paradise is the golden age of the past, as many legends in other cultures also see it. The messianic time is the golden age of the future. The two ages are the same, inasmuch as they are a state of harmony. They are different, inasmuch as the first state of harmony existed only by virtue of man's *not yet* having been born, while the new state of harmony exists as a result of man's having been fully born. The messianic time is the return to innocence, and at the same time it is no return at all, because it is the goal toward which man strives after having lost his innocence.

The word "messiah" literally means "the anointed one," in the sense of designating the expected redeemer, and does not occur in this sense either in the Hebrew Bible or in the books of the Apocrypha. In some of the prophets (Nahum, Zephaniah, Habakkuk, Malachi, Joel, and Daniel) there is no human messiah at all, and the Lord alone is the redeemer. In others, there is only a collective messiah, and not an individual one; the collective messiah is the kingdom of the House of David (the "saviors" of Amos, Ezekiel, Obadiah). In Haggai and Zechariah it is an actual person, Zerubbabel of the House of David. In Jeremiah there is the concept of a "king," or God himself as the redeemer. The first Isaiah speaks of the "end of days," in which God himself will judge among the nations and in which "a rod out of the stem of Jesse" will be the judge (King); the second Isaiah speaks of the "redeemer." In other prophets we find also the idea of a "new covenant"; in Hosea particularly, one between man and all of nature (animals and plants).

In Micah God himself will be the judge and redeemer. The word "messiah" in the sense of redeemer is employed for the first time in the pseudepigraphic book of Enoch, probably around the time of Herod the Great. It is only after the Jews had lost their kingdom and their king that the personification of the messianic time in the figure of the anointed king becomes popular.

The political situation in which the prophets lived, and their personal characteristics, influence their concepts, their hopes, and their protests. Many emphasize the day of the Lord (later called the Day of Judgment), as the day of punishment which precedes repentance and redemption. According to some prophets (Amos, Hosea, Second Isaiah, Malachi), punishment is brought only upon Israel; according to others (Nahum, Habbakuk, Obadiah, Haggai, first and second Zechariah, Daniel), upon the Gentiles alone; and according to all other prophets, judgment comes upon Israel *and* the Gentiles alike. While for some the judgment is righteous punishment for the sinner, for most prophets (for instance, Hosea, Jeremiah, the second Isaiah) it is primarily moral improvement. While some (for instance, Amos, Micah, Zephaniah) prophesy a victory over the Gentiles at the time of redemption, most prophets (from Zephaniah onward) believe that redemption will come without war, and hardly speak of victory. It must be noted, however, that one finds in the same prophet (for instance, in Micah) visions of the punishment of the Gentiles, together with the messianic vision of universal brotherhood and peace among all nations. Certain elements, such as the war against Gog, prince of Magog, are found only in Ezekiel, while only in Daniel do we find the idea of a general resurrection of the dead in which the good will awaken to everlasting life, and the evil to everlasting darkness.

While one cannot speak of a straight line in the evolution of prophetic thought from the earliest to the later prophets, it is nevertheless possible to say that from the first Isaiah onward, the basic vision of the messianic time is more clearly and fully expressed than before. Perhaps its most important aspect is peace. When man has overcome the split that separates him from his fellow man and from nature—then he will indeed be at peace with those from whom he was separated. In order to have peace man must first find at-onement; peace is the result of a change within man in which union has replaced alienation. Thus the idea of peace, in the prophetic view, cannot be separated from the idea of the realization of man's humanity. Peace is more than not-war; it is harmony and union between men, it is the overcoming of separateness and alienation.

The prophetic concept of peace transcends the realm of human relations; the new harmony is also one between man and nature. Peace between man and nature is *harmony* between man and nature. Man is not threatened by nature and stops striving to dominate it; he becomes natural, and nature becomes human. He and nature cease to be opponents and become one. Man is at home in the natural world, and nature becomes a part of the human world; this is peace in the prophetic sense. (The Hebrew word for peace, *shalom,* which could best be translated as "completeness," points in the same direction.)

This state of man's peace with nature and the end of all destructiveness finds one of its supreme expressions in the famous passage of Isaiah:

> The wolf shall dwell with the lamb, and the leopard shall lie down with the kid, and the calf and the lion and the fatling together, and a little child shall lead them.
> The cow and the bear shall feed; their young shall lie down together; and the lion shall eat straw like the ox.
> The sucking child shall play over the hole of the asp, and the weaned child shall put his hand on the adder's den.
> They shall not hurt or destroy in all my holy mountain;

for the earth shall be full of the knowledge of the Lord
as the waters cover the sea.

Isaiah 11:6–9

The idea of man's new harmony with nature in the
messianic time signifies not only the end of the struggle of
man against nature, but also that nature will not withhold
itself from man; it will become the all-loving, nurturing
mother. Nature within man will cease to be crippled, and
nature outside of man will cease to be sterile. As Isaiah
put it:

Then the eyes of the blind shall be opened, and the
ears of the deaf unstopped; then shall the lame man leap
like a hart, and the tongue of the dumb sing for joy. For
waters shall break forth in the wilderness, and streams in
the desert; the burning sand shall become a pool, and the
thirsty ground springs of water; the haunt of jackals shall
become a swamp, the grass shall become reeds and rushes.

And a highway shall be there, and it shall be called
the Holy Way; the unclean shall not pass over it, and
fools shall not err therein. No lion shall be there, nor
shall any ravenous beast come up on it; they shall not be
found there, but the redeemed shall walk there. And the
ransomed of the Lord shall return, and come to Zion
with singing; everlasting joy shall be upon their heads;
they shall obtain joy and gladness, and sorrow and sighing
shall flee away.

Isaiah 35:5–10

Or, as the second Isaiah puts it:
"Behold, I am doing a new thing; now it springs forth,

do you not perceive it? I will make a way in the wilderness and rivers in the desert. The wild beasts will honor me, the jackals and the ostriches; for I give water in the wilderness, rivers in the desert, to give drink to my chosen people" (Is. 43:19–20).

Hosea expresses the idea of a new covenant between man and all animals and plants, and between all men: "And I will make for you a covenant on that day with the beasts of the field, the birds of the air, and the creeping things of the ground; and I will abolish the bow, the sword, and war from the land; and I will make you lie down in safety" (Hosea 2:18).

The idea of peace among men finds its culmination in the prophetic concept of the destruction of all weapons of war as expressed, among others, by Micah: "He shall judge between many peoples, and shall decide for strong nations afar off; and they shall beat their swords into plowshares, and their spears into pruning hooks; nation shall not lift up sword against nation, neither shall they learn war any more; but they shall sit every man under his vine and under his fig tree, and none shall make them afraid; for the mouth of the Lord of hosts has spoken" (Micah 4:3–4).

Life, says the prophet, will triumph over death. Metal, instead of being used for the spilling of blood, will open the womb of Mother Earth to permit life to grow. Another aspect of the messianic time shines clearly through Micah's prophecy: not only will war disappear, but also fear; or rather, war can disappear only when nobody has the wish and the power to make another afraid. Furthermore, not even may one specific concept of God be demanded: "For all the peoples walk each in the name of its god" (Micah 4:5). Religious fanaticism, the source of so much strife and

destruction, will have disappeared. When peace and freedom
from fear have been established, it will matter little which
thought concepts mankind uses to give expression to its
supreme goals and values.

Closely related to this is the universalistic aspect of the
messianic time. Men will not only cease to destroy each other,
man will have overcome the experience of separateness between one nation and another. Once he has achieved being
fully human the stranger ceases to be a stranger; the illusion
of essential differences between nation and nation disappears
and there are no longer any "chosen" people. As Amos puts
it: " 'Are you not like the Ethiopians to me, O people of
Israel?' says the Lord. 'Did I not bring up Israel from the
land of Egypt, and the Philistines from Caphtor and the
Syrians from Kir?' " (Amos 9:7)

The idea that all nations are to be equally loved by God
and that there is no favorite son is beautifully expressed
also by Isaiah: "In that day there will be a highway from
Egypt to Assyria, and the Assyrian will come into Egypt,
and the Egyptian into Assyria, and the Egyptian will worship
with the Assyrians. In that day Israel will be the third with
Egypt and Assyria, a blessing in the midst of the earth, whom
the Lord of hosts has blessed, saying, 'Blessed be Egypt my
people, and Assyria the work of my hands, and Israel my
heritage' " (Is. 19:23–25).

An essential aspect of the prophets' messianic teaching
is their attitude toward power and force. Indeed, we must
admit that all human history so far (perhaps with the exception of certain primitive societies) has been based on force:
the force and power of a prosperous minority over a
majority who work hard and enjoy little. In order to uphold
the rule of force, the minds of the people had to be dis-

torted in such a way that both the rulers and the ruled believed that their situation, as it existed, had been decreed by God, by nature, or by moral law. The prophets are revolutionaries who rob force and power of their moral and religious disguises. Their motto in foreign policy is: "Not by might, nor by power, but by my Spirit [is history made] says the Lord of hosts" (Zech. 4:6). They speak against the folly of relying on foreign powers and alliances. As Hosea says: "Assyria shall not save us, we will not ride upon horses; and we will say no more, 'Our God,' to the work of our hands. In thee the orphan finds mercy" (Hosea 14:3).

In this statement Hosea has brought together three elements which are seemingly distinct, and yet which form only three aspects of the same phenomenon: the futility of secular power for the survival of the nation, the futility of idols, and the concept of God as one who has compassion for the orphan. The orphan, the widow, the poor, and the stranger are those members of society who have no power. The prophetic demand for justice is in their behalf, and the prophetic protest is directed against the rich and powerful— both kings and priests.*

The underlying ethical-religious conviction of the prophets is seen in a beautiful passage from the second Isaiah which is directed against an empty ritualism:

> Cry aloud, spare not, lift up your voice like a trumpet; declare to my people their transgression, to the house of Jacob their sins. Yet they seek me daily, and delight to know my ways, as if they were a nation that did righteousness and did not forsake the ordinance of their God;

* Cf. Is. 5:18–23.

they ask of me righteous judgments, they delight to draw near to God. "Why have we fasted, and thou seest it not? Why have we humbled ourselves, and thou takest no knowledge of it?" Behold, in the day of your fast you seek your own pleasure, and oppress all your workers. Behold, you fast only to quarrel and to fight and to hit with wicked fist. Fasting like yours this day will not make your voice to be heard on high. Is such the fast that I choose, a day for a man to humble himself? Is it to bow down his head like a rush, and to spread sackcloth and ashes under him? Will you call this a fast, and a day acceptable to the Lord?

Is not this the fast that I choose: to loose the bonds of wickedness, to undo the thongs of the yoke, to let the oppressed go free, and to break every yoke? Is it not to share your bread with the hungry, and bring the homeless poor into your house; when you see the naked, to cover him, and not to hide yourself from your own flesh? Then shall your light break forth like the dawn, and your healing shall spring up speedily; your righteousness shall go before you, the glory of the Lord shall be your rear guard. Then you shall call, and the Lord will answer: you shall cry, and he will say, Here I am.

If you take away from the midst of you the yoke, the pointing of the finger, and speaking wickedness, if you pour yourself out for the hungry and satisfy the desire of the afflicted, then shall your light rise in the darkness and your gloom be as the noonday.

Isaiah 58:1–10

The following part of a speech by Jeremiah shows the same spirit:

You recently repented and did what was right in my eyes by proclaiming liberty, each to his neighbor, and you made a covenant before me in the house which is called by my name; but then you turned around and profaned my name when each of you took back his male and female slaves, whom you had set free according to their desire, and you brought them into subjection to be your slaves. Therefore, thus says the Lord: You have not obeyed me by proclaiming liberty, every one to his brother and to his neighbor; behold, I proclaim to you liberty to the sword, to pestilence, and to famine, says the Lord. I will make you a horror to all the kingdoms of the earth. And the men who transgressed my covenant and did not keep the terms of the covenant which they made before me, I will make like the calf which they cut in two and passed between its parts—the princes of Judah, the princes of Jerusalem, the eunuchs, the priests, and all the people of the land who passed between the parts of the calf; and I will give them into the hand of their enemies and into the hand of those who seek their lives. Their dead bodies shall be food for the birds of the air and the beasts of the earth. And Zedekiah king of Judah, and his princes I will give into the hand of their enemies and into the hand of those who seek their lives, into the hand of the army of the king of Babylon which has withdrawn from you. Behold, I will command, says the Lord, and will bring them back to this city; and they will fight against it, and take it, and burn it with fire. I will make the cities of Judah a desolation without inhabitant.

                                        Jeremiah 34:15–22

The prophets opposed a corrupt priesthood allied with corrupt kings and princes; they spoke in the name of the God of justice and love, and they foretold the downfall of the state and of priestly power. They did not compromise with expediency, nor hide their attack behind courteous words. No wonder that in their time they were reviled by the mob, and some of them were exiled, jailed, or killed by the priests and kings. Only many generations later were these men who had dared to speak vindicated by the course of history, by the downfall of all those who had believed that the sword and mighty idols could guarantee their existence.

4 Post-Biblical Development of the Messianic Concept

In the prophetic literature the messianic vision rested upon the tension between "what existed and was still there and that which was becoming and was yet to be." * In the postprophetic period a change takes place in the meaning of the messianic idea, making its first appearance in the Book of Daniel around 164 B.C. While in the prophets the aim of human evolution lies in the *Yamim ha-baim*, in "the days to come," or *be-aharit ha-yamim*, "the end of the days," in Daniel and in part of the apocalyptic literature following him the aim is *ha-olam ha-ba*, the "world to come." This "world to come" is not a world *within* history but an ideal world *above*, a world in the beyond. In the prophetic vision "the expected one, the object of longing is a scion of the House of David who will *fulfill* history; here he has become the supernatural being who descends from the heavenly heights to *end* history. There, in the prophetic world, the line of longing is horizontal; here—and this is the essence of the apocalyptic orientation—it is vertical." † We find here the differentiation which is to become later the crucial

* L. Baeck, *op. cit.*, p. 31.
† L. Baeck, *ibid.*, p. 31. [My italics, E. F.]

difference between the Jewish and the Christian development. The Jewish development emphasizes the horizontal,
the Christian development emphasizes the vertical axis.*
The book of Daniel became the pattern for a new kind
of literature which flourished from the middle of the
second century B.C. to the middle of the second century A.D.
This literature, strongly influenced by Alexandrian Hellenistic philosophy, assumes an ideal realm beyond this world
where all truly important things have their place: the Bible,
the Temple, the people of Israel, and the messiah. They
were created by God before the world of becoming. The
messiah thus becomes he that was from the beginning. The
resurrection of the dead and then eternal life become the
content of apocalyptic hopes.

However, this "vertical" idea of salvation never takes
the place of the "horizontal" prophetic vision of the messianic time. They both exist side by side, from the apocalyptical literature to the rabbinical expectations about the messiah.
Furthermore, in spite of the great difference between a this-
worldly, historical and an otherworldly, transhistorical salvation, one important factor is common to both ideas of salva-

* It is very interesting that Teilhard de Chardin many years later
used terms quite similar to those used by Leo Baeck. Teilhard de
Chardin speaks of the Christian faith as "aspiring upward, in a
personal transcendency toward the Highest" and of "human faith,"
driving forward to see the ultrahuman; these correspond to Baeck's
"vertical axis" and "horizontal" line. Teilhard de Chardin himself
proposes a "rectified" Christian faith "reconciling the two: salvation
. . . at once Upward and Forward in a Christ who is both Savior and
Mover not only of individual men, but of anthropogenesis as a
whole." (*The Future of Man* [New York: Harper & Row, 1965], pp.
263–269.) Such a blending between both directions can be found in the
Apocryphal and Talmudic literature. Teilhard de Chardin in his
concept of "driving forward," however, does not refer to the Jewish
concept of messianism but to Marxist humanism.

tion: salvation is not individual but collective; it is either a new historical period or the cataclysmic end of all history. In both cases it refers to a change in the situation of mankind, rather than to a change in the fate of one individual.

Different books of the apocalyptical literature vary in their respective emphases on the historical and purely spiritual concept of messianism. In the earlier parts of the Book of Enoch (around 110 B.C.) the messianic age begins with the destruction of the wicked and the sinners on the day of the great judgment. The elect will live and never sin again, and they will complete their days in peace. The entire earth will be filled with righteousness, and nature will be all-abundant. (Similar descriptions can be found also in the apocalypse of the Syriac Baruch, in the tradition of one of the oldest Church Fathers, Papias, as preserved in the writings of Irenaeus and in the sayings of the early Tannaim.)

In the Book of Enoch, as in other apocalyptic writings and in rabbinical sources, one concept plays a very important role—that of "the birth pangs of messiah." Whether these "birth pangs" consist of a destructive war of Gog and Magog or a state of social and moral anarchy, of earthquakes, or of utter hopelessness, they always have the function of leading to repentance, and repentance is the condition for redemption, for the arrival of the messianic time. This concept of the "birth pangs of the messiah" as the condition for the arrival of the messianic time is also found in many of the later rabbinical writings.

In other pseudepigraphic books, like the Fourth Book of Ezra (around 100 B.C.), the heavenly Jerusalem will appear and the messiah will be revealed. The messiah and the righteous shall live in joy for four hundred years;

then all will die and the world will return to primeval silence, as it was in the beginning. After this period of silence a new world will emerge, the "world to come." Previous history, in this concept, is the forerunner of the messianic age; the messianic age is the forerunner of the world to come, the world which transcends history. In some of these writings the difference between the messianic age and the world to come is strictly emphasized, while in others there is some confusion. On the whole, the apocryphal literature is centered around the sequence "the birth pangs of the messiah" (punishment) → repentance → the days of the messiah → the day of judgment → the resurrection of the dead → the world to come (*ha-olam ha-ba*). The historical and the metaphysical concepts are blended in this way, although depending on varying historical circumstances, sometimes the one, sometimes the other aspect is emphasized.

The apocryphal literature constitutes the transition from the biblical to the rabbinical phase of the Jewish tradition. The first part of this rabbinical tradition is the period of the Tannaim, the more authoritative teachers who complete the Mishnah, roughly about A.D. 200; the second part is the period of the Amoraim and Geonim who lived in Palestine and in Babylonia. The older sages, who lived under the Hasmonean kings, found themselves mostly in opposition to these worldly representatives of Jewish nationalism, and hence the idea of national independence as such was not particularly appealing to them. They had seen it under the Hasmoneans and recognized that it did not further the aims of the prophetic concept of the messianic time. This may be the reason why the Tannaim did not say much about the messianic age. While their greatest representatives had no love for Rome, national independence and the Temple with all its rituals were of secondary importance to the study and the observance of the law. As I pointed out before, when the Romans destroyed the Temple and the last remnants of Jewish political independence in A.D. 70, they destroyed a façade behind which a new scene had already arisen, that of rabbinical Judaism, a religion without a temple, sacrifices, priests; a religion also without theological dogmas, but exclusively concerned with right action in all aspects of life, expressive of, and conducive to, man's self-transformation into the full image of God. The Talmudic sages did not forget the Temple, they did not denounce the priestly sacrifice as sham—as the prophets had often done—but they transformed the Temple and national independence into mere symbols of the messianic time.

Just as views differ within the apocryphal books, so the Tannaim, as well as the Amoraim, differ greatly among themselves. What is common to all their views about the messianic time, however, is that it is of *this* world and not a realm transcending it. Their views were colored by political events. At the height of the cruel religious persecution by the Romans in the second century A.D., one of the greatest figures among the Tannaim, R. Akiba, who had been a universalist all his life, changed his views and believed the claim of the nationalist leader Bar Kokhba (Son of a Star) to be the messiah. Other Tannaim, however, who were contemporaries of R. Akiba, did not follow him in his illusion. They were firm in their belief that the time of the messiah had not yet arrived and that Bar Koziba (Son of Lies, as he was later called) was nothing but an impostor. On the other hand, later on, after the center of Jewish culture had moved from Palestine to

Babylonia, and when Roman oppression was no longer a
reality, the vivid colors that the picture of the messianic
time had for the prophets and the apocryphal literature is
lost for some Amoraim. On the whole, however, the messianic
age retains its color throughout the centuries following the
fall of the Temple.

There were various views among the rabbis, but one
element was held in common: the messiah is never the
"savior"; he does not transform man, nor change his substance. The messiah is always a symbol, the anointed king
from the House of David, who will make his appearance
when the time has come. In this very fact that the messiah
is a symbol of a new *historical* period, and not a savior, lies
one decisive difference between the Jewish concept and the
one developed by the Christian Church.

The narrowest concept of the messiah can be found in
the idea that "this world differs from [that of] the days of
the messiah only in respect of servitude to [foreign]
powers" * (that is, that the Jews will no longer be oppressed
politically). While this concept of political emancipation
is also found in some of the prophetic utterances, it lacks the
element of universal historical transformation which forms
the central point of the prophetic messianic vision.

But in most Talmudic statements the idea of political
emancipation goes together with that of religious and
spiritual redemption. The messiah will re-establish the
national independence of the Jews and rebuild the Temple—
at the same time he will establish the kingdom of God in
the whole world, root out idolatry, put an end to sin.†

* Sanhedrin 99a. (The same view was also accepted by Maimonides, *Mishneh Torah*, XIV, 5, 12.)
† Cf. Joseph Klausner, *op. cit.*, p. 392.

The messiah in the Talmudic concept will be a man of purely human origin, even though one source states that his name is one of the seven things which "were created before the world was created" (Pesahim 54a). (The other six are: the Torah, repentance, the Garden of Eden, Gehenna, the Throne of Glory, and the temple.) He will bring peace and "will not open his mouth except for peace, as it is written [Is. 52:7] 'How beautiful upon the mountains are the feet of the messenger of good tidings, that announceth peace.' " * He is a man of justice; in fact, he can "smell" what is right and what is wrong. Thus a Talmudic source says, "Bar Koziba [Bar Kokhba] reigned two and a half years and then said to the rabbis, 'I am the messiah.' They answered, 'Of messiah it is written that he smells and judges; let us see whether he [Bar Koziba] can do so.' When they saw that he was unable to judge by the scent, they slew him."

About the state of man in the messianic age we find a very interesting Talmudic statement: "[In the messianic era] there is neither merit nor guilt" (Shabbat 151b). For man in the messianic time, so seems to be the idea in this statement, the problem of guilt will disappear; but with this disappears also the problem of good works. He does not need good works in order to justify himself—because he has become fully himself.

What are the preconditions for the messianic time, according to the Talmudic sources? There are actually two opposite ideas regarding the condition required for the coming of the messiah. One is that the messiah will come only when suffering and evil have reached such a degree that men will repent and thus be ready. There are numerous

* Derek Eretz Zuta, Chap. II (Section on peace); quoted by J. Klausner, *op. cit.*, p. 521.

descriptions of this catastrophic situation which occur before the final historical change. The following statements are characteristic: "Thus has R. Yohanan said: In the generation when the son of David [the messiah] will come, scholars will be few in number, and as for the rest, their eyes will fail through sorrow and grief. Multitudes of trouble and evil decrees will be promulgated anew, each new evil coming with haste before the other has ended" (Sanhedrin 97a). Or: " 'It has been taught,' R. Nehemiah said, 'In the generation of messiah's coming, impudence will increase, esteem be perverted, the vine yield its fruit, yet shall wine be dear, and the kingdom will be converted to heresy with none to rebuke them.' This supports R. Isaac, who said: 'The son of David will not come until the whole world is converted to the beliefs of the heretics' " (Sanhedrin 97a).*

The other concept is that the messiah will come, not after catastrophes, but as the result of man's own continuous improvement. This is the meaning of the following statement: "If Israel were to keep two Sabbaths according to the laws thereof, they would be redeemed immediately" (Shabbat 118b). Here the full keeping of one command (one, to be sure, which in itself refers to the Sabbath as the anticipation of the messianic time) would already be sufficient to bring the messiah without any need for previous suffering. In other utterances the condition for the coming of the messiah is expressed in the negative form by saying that his coming depends on Israel's capacity to renounce sin. This is the meaning of the following passage: "Why has

* There is a striking parallel between this concept and Marx's idea that the working class, precisely because it is the most alienated and suffering, is the most revolutionary class, destined to bring about a radical change in the world.

not the messiah come? [Answer] Now today is the Day of
Atonement and yet how many virgins were embraced in
Nehardea?" (Yoma 19a) Or we hear that "The messiah will
not come until there are no more conceited men in Israel,"
or "until all judges and officers are gone from Israel," or that
"Jerusalem will be redeemed only by righteousness" (Sanhedrin 98a).

The same idea, that redemption depends on the slow
process of perfection by the people themselves, is very clearly
expressed in the following saying: "Rab said: 'All the
predestined dates [for redemption] have passed and the
matter [now] depends only on repentance and good deeds"
(Sanhedrin 97b).

The idea that the arrival of the messiah depends on the
readiness of Israel, that is, on its moral and spiritual progress,
rather than on catastrophes, is also expressed in the following
Talmudic story:

R. Joshua ben Levi asked Elijah "When will the messiah
come?"

"Go and ask him himself," was his reply.

"Where is he sitting?"

"At the entrance" [at the gates of the town, or, according to the Vilna Gaon, of Rome].

"And by what sign may I recognize him?"

"He is sitting among the poor lepers: all of them untie
[the bandages of their sores for dressing] all at once,
and rebandage them together [they first take off all the
bandages and treat each sore and then replace them to-
gether], whereas he unties and bandages them separately
[before treating the next], thinking, should I be wanted
[it being time for my appearance as the messiah] I must

not be delayed [through having to bandage a number of sores]."

So he went to him and greeted him [the messiah], saying: "Peace upon thee, Master and Teacher."

"Peace upon thee, son of Levi," he replied.

"When wilt thou come, Master?" asked he.

"Today," was his answer.

On his returning to Elijah, the latter inquired, "What did he say to thee?" . . .

"He spoke falsely to me," he rejoined, "he stated that he would come today but has not."

He [Elijah] answered him, "This is what he said to thee, *Today, if you will hear his voice*" (Ps. 95:7).

Sanhedrin 98a

The story insists that the messiah does not bring salvation, and that salvation is not dependent on the "birth pangs of the messiah," but on the readiness of the people, provided they make the choice; hence, the messiah might appear at any minute.

There are Talmudists who say that even repentance is not a requisite for redemption. Thus Samuel responds to Rab's statement, that salvation now depends only on repentance and good deeds, by saying: "It is sufficient for a mourner to keep his [period of] mourning" (Sanhedrin 97b). (Israel's suffering in Exile in itself sufficiently warrants their redemption, regardless of repentance.) * In fact, there is a long discussion on this question, with some rabbis claiming that redemption requires repentance, while R. Joshua interprets the verse in Isaiah 52:3, "You have sold yourselves for

* Cf. my interpretation of Israel's suffering in Egypt as a sufficient condition for God's decision to liberate them (p. 93).

naught [idolatry] and ye shall be redeemed without money," as meaning "without repentance and good deeds" (Sanhedrin 97b).

Aside from the opposing views that catastrophe or growing enlightenment, respectively, will bring about redemption, a third one holds that both possibilities exist. Thus R. Yohanan taught: "The son of David [messiah] will come only in a generation that is either altogether righteous or altogether wicked" (Sanhedrin 98a). This statement emphasizes the radical nature of the views concerning the coming of the messiah. The improvement of man is not enough. He must either have achieved full humanity or he must have lost himself completely, and thus be ready for a full "return."

The hope for the coming of the messiah was not a pallid faith in a never-never time. It was the hope that sustained the Jews in their suffering and gave them courage to tolerate their humiliations without despising themselves. Without this hope, common blood, suffering, and courage would hardly have been sufficient to save the Jews from a demoralization born of hopelessness and despair. The intensity of this hope for the coming of the messiah was apparent in many ways. Perhaps this hope was expressed most clearly in periodic outbursts which ended each time in tragic disillusionment. The belief that the "heavenly kingdom" was near, or that it had already arrived, was the basis of the early Christian message; the belief that the messiah had come was the basis for the enthusiastic reception of impostors, such as Bar Kokhba in the second century A.D. But Bar Kokhba was not the last of the false messiahs.

The period between A.D. 440 and 490, according to an old tradition, was a time in which the coming of the messiah

was expected. When a Cretan Jew, Moses, declared himself
to be the messiah, the Jews of Crete—a strong Jewish settle-
ment—neglected their businesses and forsook all ordinary
pursuits of life. When the messiah, standing on a promontory
of land projecting into the sea, commanded them to throw
themselves into the ocean, as the waters would divide for them
just as the Red Sea had at the behest of Moses, they com-
plied with his command, and many of them died. Many
others, after this disappointment, subsequently embraced
Christianity.*

Before continuing with the history of the false messiahs,
it should be mentioned that during the Middle Ages learned
rabbis were often forced by the popes, kings, and other
Christian authorities to conduct disputations with Catholic
theologians, usually Jewish converts, regarding the question
whether Jesus was the messiah announced by the prophets
and the Jewish sages. Sometimes these disputations were
conducted under pleasant conditions; often there was danger
for the Jewish participants. But whatever the conditions
were, the rabbis usually showed great dignity, courage, and
skill in their attempts to refute the Christian claims. One of
the most interesting disputations took place between Nahmanides (1195–1270), one of the greatest medieval Jewish
scholars, and Pablo Christiano, a converted Jew, in Barcelona, in 1263, before the king of Aragon. Nahmanides
argued that Jesus could not have been the messiah, since
his advent had not inaugurated universal peace, which is
the characteristic feature of the messianic period as pictured
by the prophets. Turning to the king of Aragon, Nahmanides

* According to the Christian chronicles, Socrates, *Historia Ecclesi-
astica*, Vol. VII, p. 36 (Bohn's edition); quoted by J. H. Greenstone, *op. cit.*, pp. 109 ff.

exclaimed, "It behooves thee and thy knights, O King, to put an end to all warfare, as the beginning of the messianic era demands." * Nahmanides' words express the deep conviction so characteristic of prophetic and rabbinical thought, that the advent of the messiah is inseparable from eternal peace. Indeed, his words addressed to the king of Aragon are as valid today as they were then.

In 1284 Abraham Abulafia of Tudela announced his claim to messiahship and the year 1290 as the date of his messianic appearance. But a letter written by one of the great Spanish rabbinical authorities, R. Solomon ben Adret, denouncing him as an adventurer, caused his attempt to collapse almost immediately. Another adventurer, Nissim ben Abraham of Avila (Spain), claimed to be the messiah around the same time, but did not appear on the appointed date, thus disappointing many Jews who had eagerly received his message.

The appearance of the Zohar, the most important Jewish mystical work ascribed to the second-century R. Simeon ben Yohai, and allegedly discovered by the thirteenth-century kabbalistic writer Moses de León of Granada, Spain, contributed much to fanning messianic expectations.† Jewish mysticism became one of the strongest inspirations for messianic faith and often contributed to the appearance of false messiahs, though it also led to the most original development in postmedieval Jewish history: Hasidism.

* Quoted by J. H. Greenstone, *ibid.*, p. 167.

† The first Christian scholar to have translated part of the Zohar into Latin was William Postel (Paris, 1552), while Pico della Mirandola wrote a short thesis in Latin about the Zohar. Cf. *The Zohar,* translated by Harry Sperling and Maurice Simon, with an introduction by J. Abelson (London: Soncino Press, 1949). It is interesting that these two greatest humanists were among the first to become interested in the Zohar. See also *The Book of Splendor,* selected and edited by Gershom G. Scholem (New York: Schocken Books, 1949).

One of the greatest Jewish philosophers in Spain, Isaac ben Judah Abrabanel (1437–1509), swayed by kabbalistic influences, predicted the advent of the messiah for 1503 and the beginning of the messianic age for 1531, concurrent with the fall of Rome. As a result of his predictions, a German Jew, Asher Lemmlein, declared himself the forerunner of the messiah.

One of the most fantastic and astounding among the believers in the immediate advent of the messiah was Diego Pires (1501–1532), born a "New Christian." When he returned to the Jewish faith of his ancestors he called himself Solomon Molkho. He had risen to the high position of royal secretary to a high court of justice when he heard of David Reubeni. Reubeni appeared in Europe with the story that he came on behalf of his brother who was the king of a Jewish Kingdom in Chardar. He offered the Pope and Christian kings an army of 300,000 men to wrest the Holy Land from the Moslems if they would provide firearms and ships. Molkho, impressed by Reubeni, announced that the reign of the messiah would commence in 1540, and he carried his message to Jews and Gentiles. In spite of the protection of the Pope, Molkho was eventually seized by the Inquisition, together with Reubeni, and burned at the stake.

The sequence of false messiahs since Bar Kokhba found its crowning point in Sabbatai Zevi, from Smyrna, in the seventeenth century. He too claimed to be the messiah and revealed himself in 1648. He set the year 1666 as the beginning of the messianic time. Jews all over Europe were filled with the expectation that the "end of days" had arrived; many sold their houses and all their property and prepared themselves to march toward Jerusalem. This Jewish "crusade" ended in the same abysmal failure as the Bar Kokhba war. Sabbatai Zevi yielded to the threats of the sultan and became a Moslem, changing his name to Mehemed Effendi and marrying a Turkish woman. While the majority of his adherents were horrified by this act of betrayal, a hard core was not convinced even by this. On the contrary, falling back on the mystical doctrine that in order to achieve salvation man must descend to the very depth of sin, they rationalized the false messiah's betrayal as proof of his authenticity. Why else should he have committed the sin of conversion, if not to save his brethren?

While Sabbatai Zevi was the most significant of all the false messiahs, he was not the last. His immediate successor was Michael Cardozo (1630–1706), a converted marrano who proclaimed himself as the messiah. His career ended when he was killed by a nephew. In Germany, Mordecai of Eisenstadt; in Turkey, Jacob Quendo; and eventually in Galicia (Poland), Jacob Frank—all proclaimed themselves messiahs, only to fail as miserably as their predecessors.

I have enumerated the list of the false messiahs in order to demonstrate how the hope for the advent of the messiah never flagged, from the time of the destruction of the Temple to the eighteenth century. Again and again a large part of the Jewish community believed that the time of the messiah had come; this belief was so real that they sold their houses and gave up their worldly activities. They were convinced; yet every time, their hope was disappointed, leaving them in a state of shock and despair which often led to the conversion of many to the Christian faith.

Beginning in the seventeenth century the situation of the Jews began to improve in the West. Only in eastern Europe did persecution continue in its worst forms, and with it came a revival of messianic hopes. This happened most con-

spicuously in the Hasidic movement, a religious movement
springing up among the poor and unlearned masses in
Poland and Galicia during the second half of the eigtheenth
century after devastating pogroms in that area. This movement, which gave a central place to joy and religious enthusiasm rather than to rabbinical discipline and learnedness,
and which in some aspects paralleled the social composition
of the early Christians and their relationship to the Pharisees,
was filled with impatient and ardent hope for the messiah,
although it did not produce a false messiah.* Although the
role of messianic expectation within Hasidic lore is well
known, it may still be useful to quote a few examples, including among them even apologies for the false messiahs: †

An unbeliever asserted to the Rabbi of Berditschev that
the great masters of old were steeped in error. For instance,
Rabbi Akiba believed that Bar Kochba was the Messiah,
and enrolled under his banner.

Thereupon the Berditschever narrated this parable:
"Once upon a time the only son of an Emperor fell ill.
One physician advised that a piece of linen be smeared

* Maybe the fact that the movement gave origin to many small
groups, each under its own charismatic leader, accounts for this.

† Martin Buber has done the most to bring this literature to the
attention of the Western reader. Cf. also the excellent *Hasidic Anthology* by Louis L. Newman.

Scholem has emphasized that "Hasidism represents an attempt to
preserve those elements of Kabbalism which were capable of evoking
a popular response, but stripped of the messianic flavor to which
they owed their chief successes during the preceding period" (*Major
Trends,* p. 329). With all due respect for Scholem's authority, it
seems to me that the Hasidic stories quoted here—and to which many
others could be added—show that the messianic elements had not
been eliminated as much as he claims.

with a burning salve and wrapped around the bare body of the patient. Another physician, however, discouraged this, because the boy was too weak to endure the pain the salve would cause. Thereupon a third physician recommended a sleeping-draught; but a fourth physician feared this might endanger the heart of the patient. Upon this, a fifth physician advised that the sleeping-draught be given by teaspoonfuls to the patient, as often as he awakened and felt the burning of the salve. And this was done.

"Thus, when God saw that the soul of Israel was sick unto death, he wrapped it in the biting linen of poverty and misery, but laid upon it the sleep of forgetfulness, in order that it might endure the pain. However, lest the spirit expire utterly, he awakens it from hour to hour with a false hope of a Messiah, and again puts it to sleep until the night shall have passed and the true Messiah shall appear. For such reasons the eyes of the wise are sometimes blinded." *

The same spirit is expressed in the following story: "Of Sabbatai Zevi, the false Messiah and Pseudo-Redeemer of Smyrna, the Besht [founder of Hasidism] said:

" 'Many have trodden the same steep path [in the study of the kabbalah] and have attained the fortunate goal. He, too, had a holy spark in his being; he fell, however, into the net of Samael, the false deceiver, who thrust him into the role of a Redeemer. This overtook him only because of his arrogance.' " †

The following stories express the intensity of the messianic

* Quoted in Louis L. Newman, p. 250.
† Quoted in Louis L. Newman, pp. 250–251, from *Priester der Liebe* by Chaim Bloch (Vienna, 1930).

expectations among the Hasidic leaders, and even the impatience and demanding nature of this hope:

A Hasid placed this question before the Berditschever:
"Does not the verse in Malachi 3:23, which states that Elijah will appear before the great day of the Redemption to prepare the hearts of the fathers and their children, contradict the statement in Sanhedrin (98) that the Messiah replied to a query concerning the time of his advent with the verse in Psalm 95:7: "Today, if you will obey His Voice"?

The Rabbi replied: "The Messiah could come today without being preceded by Elijah, if we ourselves prepare our hearts without troubling the Prophet to do it for us. Let us make ourselves ready, then, to receive the Messiah any day by obeying the Voice of the Lord." *

A moving expression of messianic hope and impatience is the following prayer of a Hasidic leader:

Before Kol Nidrei, the Oheler stood before the Ark and said:
"Lord of the Universe! Thou art well aware of my unworthiness, but Thou also knowest that I do not speak falsehood and that now, before the advent of Yom Kippur, I wish to relate to Thee my true thoughts. Had I known that the Messiah would not come in my own days, long ago I would have surrendered my soul to Thee. All that has held me to life is my expectation that the Messiah would speedily come. Let Messiah come now, not for our

* Berger, *Esser Oroth* (Warsaw, 1913), p. 60; quoted in L. Newman, pp. 246–247.

sake, but for Thy sake, so that Thy name may be glorified.
I am prepared to die at once, if it has been decreed that
I am unworthy to behold his coming, and if my living
delays for even a moment the Redemption." *

The Riziner said: "It is required of us that we repent
and atone before redemption, but we have lost the power,
for we are staggering under the burden of our sufferings
like drunken men who cannot walk the way. Our Sages
have demanded, not in plain words, but by plain implication, redemption before atonement, when they said that
crushing poverty makes men avert their faces from a
knowledge of the Creator." †

Here is an example for the attitude that the messiah is by
no means God, but utterly human, and that his coming is
the result of the growing perfection of the people: "Said the
Stretiner: 'Each Jew has within himself an element of the
messiah which he is required to purify and mature. Messiah
will come when Israel has brought him to the perfection of
growth and purity within themselves.' " ‡

The hope for the expectation is by no means expressed in
a quiet appeal to God. It is often phrased as a demand which
tries to compel God to send the messiah:

Before his death, the Apter said: "The Berditschever declared, before he passed over into 'his world,' that, when
he arrived in Heaven, he would urgently make demands

* B. Ehrmann, *Peer ve-Khavod* (Muncats, 1912); quoted in L.
Newman, p. 249.
† Chaim Bloch, *Gemeinde der Chassidim* (Vienna, 1920); quoted
in L. Newman, p. 248.
‡ I. Berger, *Esser Tzachtzochoth* (Piotrkov, 1910); quoted in L.
Newman, p. 248.

regarding Redemption until the Messiah would be dispatched. When, however, he crossed over into the Heavenly Abode, the Angels were wise enough to place him in a Hall of the highest delights, so that the Berditschever forgot his promise. I, however, faithfully pledge myself, when I attain the Heavenly Heights, that I will not allow myself to be beguiled by pleasures, and will compel the advent of the Messiah." *

The same spirit of man's challenging God is shown in the following story:

After Yom Kippur the Berditschever called over a tailor and asked him to relate his argument with God on the day before. The tailor said:

"I declared to God: You wish me to repent of my sins, but I have committed only minor offenses; I may have kept left-over cloth, or I may have eaten in a non-Jewish home, where I worked, without washing my hands.

"But Thou, O Lord, hast committed grievous sins: Thou hast taken away babies from their mothers, and mothers from their babies. Let us be quits: mayest Thou forgive me, and I will forgive Thee."

Said the Berditschever: "Why did you let God off so easily? You might have forced Him to redeem all of Israel." †

* Chaim Bloch, *Gemeinde der Chassidim;* quoted by L. Newman, p. 247.

† I. Ashkenazy, *Otzroth Idisher Humor* (New York, 1929); quoted by L. Newman, p. 57.

5   The Paradox of Hope

In reviewing the post-biblical development of the messianic concept we have seen desperate outbursts of hope, which often led to the fatal belief in a false messiah. Even one of the greatest humanists among the sages, R. Akiba, could not withstand the seduction of the false hope; and even after Sabbatai Zevi's betrayal, there were many who could not accept the fact that he was an impostor.

The economic, social, and political hardships which the Jews had to undergo over many centuries make it easy to understand their impatience and the intensity of the wish for the coming of the messiah. But the disillusionments made them also more aware of the danger of being carried away by one's hopes and wishes. The rabbinical literature gave warning again and again against trying to "force the messiah." We find repeated warnings against any attempt to expect the messiah at a fixed date as a result of various kinds of calculations. Thus R. Jose said: "He who attempts to give the end [that is, to predict the coming of the messiah] has no chance in the world to come [strongest expression of censure]" (Megillah 3a). Or, "R. Samuel ben Nahman said in the name of Jonathan: Blasted be the bones of those who calculate the end [the messiah's advent]. For they would say, since the predetermined time has arrived, and yet he has not come, he will never come. But [even so] wait for him, as it is written, 'though he tarry, wait for him' " (Sanhedrin 97b).

This saying expresses clearly the Talmudic attitude: one must not "force the messiah," but one must expect him each minute. The attitude required is neither one of rash impatience nor of passive waiting; it is one of *dynamic hope.*

This hope is, indeed, paradoxical. It implies an attitude which visualizes salvation occurring right at this moment, yet it also is ready to accept the fact that salvation may not come in one's own lifetime, and maybe not for many generations to come. To accept this paradox of hope is not easy, as the acceptance of any kind of paradox is never easy. The natural tendency is to tear apart the two conflicting sides of a paradox. Hope without the expectation of its immediate fulfillment in the here and now deteriorates into a passive waiting; the desired goal is postponed into the remote future and loses all force.* This deterioration of hope into a passive waiting can be observed in many religions and political movements. The second coming of Christ, while still hoped for by a believing Christian, nevertheless has become an expectation for the distant future in the experience of most Christians. The same thing happened with regard to the coming of the messiah among those Jewish circles that lived in relative comfort and ease, whether it was in Babylonia, or in Germany around the beginning of the present century. When hope loses its immediacy, it tends to become alienated. The future is transformed into a goddess whom I worship, and to whom I submit. My faith is transferred to the idol: posterity. This phenomenon of the alienation of hope and the idolization of the future is very clearly expressed in the thought of Diderot and Robespierre. A random example is Robespierre's speech before the Jacobin Club on the war with Austria; he ended his speech with the following invocation:

* This type of hope is expressed in the Spanish *esperar*, which means at the same time "to hope" and "to wait." On the other hand, dynamic hope is expressed in the Hebrew word for hope, *tikvah*, the root meaning of which is "tension," like the tension of the bow with the arrow.

O posterity, sweet and tender hope of humanity, thou art not a stranger to us; it is for thee that we brave all the blows of tyranny; it is thy happiness which is the price of our painful struggles; often discouraged by the obstacles that surround us, we feel the need of thy consolations; it is to thee that we confide the task of completing our labors, and the destiny of all the unborn generations of men! . . . May the martyrs of liberty occupy in thy memory the place which the heroes of imposture and aristocracy have usurped in ours; . . . may thy first impulse be to scorn traitors and hate tyrants; may thy motto be: protection, love, benevolence to the unhappy, eternal war to oppressors! Make haste, O posterity, to bring to pass the hour of equality, of justice, of happiness! *

From Robespierre's worship of posterity to the distorted version of Marx's thought which Stalin popularized is only a small step.† For Stalin "the laws of history" were what "posterity" was for Robespierre and Diderot. Stalin's "Marxism" developed the theory that the laws of history (as interpreted by Stalin) decide on the righteous and the moral value of an action. All measures which are in line with the

---

* C. Vellay, *Discours et Rapports de Robespierre* (1908); quoted by C. L. Becker, *The Heavenly City* (New Haven, Conn.: Yale University Press, 1932), pp. 142–143. Cf. also Diderot's statements quoted by Becker, p. 149. Becker comments quite rightly, "The ideas, the phrases, are essentially religious, essentially Christian: for the worship of God, Diderot has substituted respect for posterity; for the hope of immortality in heaven, the hope of living in the memory of future generations."

† Marx himself never succumbed to the danger of idolizing the future or history. He sharply criticized those who spoke of "history" as doing this or doing that. "History," he said, "does nothing," for it is man who does and acts.

laws of history politically are morally justified; those not in line with the laws of history are "reactionary" and evil. Marx and Engels, in the middle of the nineteenth century, Lenin from 1917 to 1923, believed that the "Kingdom of Heaven," the great world revolution, was near.*

What happens as a result of the great disillusionment is similar, both in the religious and in the political spheres. When the expected salvation fails to occur, the hope that it will occur eventually is not given up explicitly, but it is asserted that salvation has already taken place in a certain provisional sense. This shift is combined with the building of an organization which itself becomes the carrier of salvation. In the Christian development, the Church became the instrument of salvation; those who joined her were individually saved by their adherence, even though the second coming of Christ would eventually affect all of mankind. When Lenin's expectation proved to be futile, the Communist party under Stalin claimed that it anticipated the great revolution; and to be a member of the party became a substitute for the hope that had failed. Eventually the party was forced to claim that socialism had been realized, although nothing of the kind had happened.

* Trotsky is perhaps the most dramatic and tragic figure midway between the positions of illusionary and rational faith. He saw with all clarity that Stalin's Soviet Union was not the fulfillment of Socialist hopes. Yet, until the day of his death he could not concede that the hope had failed completely. With all the force of his intellect he constructed theories about the Soviet Union as a "corrupt workers' state," but still "a workers' state," which it was a Communist's duty to defend in the Second World War. Lenin died at the moment when total disillusionment began to be unavoidable; Trotsky was murdered fifteen years later, on the orders of the man who had to wipe out the last remnants of the revolutionary past, in order to build his fraudulent facsimile of socialism.

The position of "the paradox of hope" is one of "faith," faith in the sense of certainty based on the inner experience of the goal, even though it has not yet been reached, and no proof exists that it ever will be. Such faith will never be possible in a spectator who "waits and sees" what will happen. It is possible only for one who with all his energy is tensed toward the goal, and whose faith is not dependent on the fact that the ideal has appeared in the flesh. Hence for the person of faith, defeat is no proof invalidating his faith, while victory will always be looked upon with suspicion, since it might turn out to be the mask for defeat. This concept of paradoxical hope has been expressed in a short statement in the Mishnah: "It is not up to you to finish the task, but you have also no right to withdraw from it" (R. Tarfon in Pirkei Avot II, 21).

v *The Concept of*
SIN AND
REPENTANCE

The Bible leaves no doubt that it does not consider man
either good or evil, but endowed with both tendencies. As I
have pointed out before, God's command not to eat of the
forbidden fruit of knowledge was a consequence, as far as
God is concerned, of his jealous concern that man might become like him. All that Adam can be reproached with is
disobedience; if disobedience is sin, then, indeed, Adam and
Eve sinned. Yet it is very significant that in the story of the
"fall" the Bible never calls Adam's act a sin.

Yet we find in the Old Testament the view that man is
endowed with "evil imaginings," with a tendency for evil.
In the Pentateuch this locution is used several times. For

159

instance, in the story of the generation of Noah the text says: "The Lord saw that . . . every imagination of the thoughts of his heart was only evil continually" (Gen. 6:5). After the flood we read: "And when the Lord smelled the pleasing odor [of Noah's burnt offerings], the Lord said in his heart, 'I will never again curse the ground because of man, for the imagination of man's heart is evil from his youth; neither will I ever again destroy every living creature as I have done'" (Gen. 8:21). A third reference reads: "And when many evils and troubles have come upon them, this song shall confront them as a witness (for it will live unforgotten in the mouths of their descendants); for I know the purposes which they are already forming, before I have brought them into the land that I swore to give" (Deut. 31:21).

None of the three references speaks of man as being essentially corrupt, but as having a *striving* for evil. The first reference is made only with regard to the generation of Noah; the second is made in order to explain God's will not to repeat the punishment meted out against Noah's generation; in fact, God's compassion is based on this deep knowledge of man's tendency for evil. The third reference is to man's evil tendencies, which continue to operate in the future.

Let us note first the interesting term which the Bible uses for the evil impulse: it is called *yetzer*. The word *yetzer* is derived from the root *YZR*, which means "to form," "to fashion" (like the potter the clay vessel). The noun *yetzer* means "form," "frame," "purpose," and, with reference to the mind, "imagination," "device," "purpose." * The term *yetzer* thus means "imaginings" (evil or good). It corresponds to what we would call "drive." The significant point

* Cf. W. Gesenius, *Hebrew and English Lexicon* (Oxford: Clarendon Press, 1910).

is that the Hebrew word indicates the important fact that evil (or good) impulses are possible only on the basis of that which is specifically human: imagination. For this very reason, only man—and not animals—can be evil or good. An animal can act in a manner which appears to us cruel (for instance, a cat playing with a mouse), but there is no evil in this play, since it is nothing but the manifestation of the animal's instinct. The problem of good and evil arises only when there is imagination. Furthermore, man can become more evil and more good because he feeds his imagination with thoughts of either evil or good. What he feeds, grows; and hence, evil and good grow or decrease. They grow precisely because of that specifically human quality—imagination.

That the Bible does not refrain from acknowledging the evil in man becomes quite clear in its descriptions of even its most important personalities. Adam was a coward; Cain is irresponsible; Noah is a weakling; Abraham allows his wife to be violated because of his fear; Jacob participates in the fraud against his brother Esau; Joseph is an ambitious manipulator; and the greatest of the Hebrew heroes, King David, commits unforgivable crimes.

Does all this not imply that the biblical view of man is that his essence is evil, that man is essentially corrupt? This interpretation cannot stand against the fact that, while the Bible acknowledges the fact of man's "evil imaginings," it also believes in his inherent capacity for good. Israel is called a "holy nation," using the same expression "holy" for the people as is used for God. While the kings commit crimes, the prophets protest against these crimes. The very prophets who castigate the kings and the people for their evilness proclaim the faith in man's capacity to follow his good inclinations and forsake evil. Isaiah (1:18) says: "Come now, let us reason together, says the Lord: though your sins are like scarlet, they shall be as white as snow; though they are red like crimson, they shall become like wool." Or, "the crooked will become straight." They teach that there is nothing inherently evil in man's nature that would prevent him from choosing the good which is in him as a potentiality, just as is the evil.

If it is true that the "evil drive" is possible only after man has emerged from the original unity with nature and has acquired self-awareness and imagination, it follows that only man can sin, can regress, can lose himself. In the Jewish view man is born with the capacity to sin, but he can return, find himself, and redeem himself by his own effort and without an act of grace from God. The Talmud summed up this view thus: "If God created the evil inclinations, he also created the Torah as its antidote [lit: spices]" (Baba Batra, 16a).

Man, in the biblical and post-biblical view, is given the choice between his "good and evil drives." In its shortest and yet most succinct form this idea of choice is expressed in the statement in Deuteronomy (30:19): "I call heaven and earth to witness against you this day, that I have set before you life and death, blessing and curse; choose life, that you and your descendants may live." * This verse makes quite clear that the Hebrews can choose between life and death, good and evil, and that there is no force which compels

---

* I have altered the text of the *Revised Standard Version* by omitting the word "therefore" before "choose life"; this word is not in the Hebrew original, and I do not see any reason to put it there, although the *vav* preceding the verb can be translated in many ways.

them, or even inclines them, to choose the one in preference to the other. All that God does is to show them the alternative and admonish them to choose life and the good.*

We find the same offer of alternatives in an earlier chapter in Deuteronomy (11:26–28). "Behold, I set before you this day a blessing and a curse: the blessing, if you obey the commandments of the Lord your God, which I command you this day, and the curse, if you do not obey the commandments of the Lord your God, but turn aside from the way which I command you this day, to go after other gods which you have not known." Here, as in the passage quoted previously, the choice between blessing and curse is man's, but these verses also define the concrete choice with which man is confronted: that of obeying God's commands or of not obeying them. Disobedience is stated in terms of worshiping the local idols, indicating again—as we have emphasized before—that the one central sin according to the Bible is that of idol worship.

The choice between blessing and curse is formulated in its most explicit and dramatic form in Deuteronomy 28. In the first part of this chapter a beautiful and rich life is promised if the people will obey God's commands. In the second part, the tragic consequences are described if the people will not obey God's commands. Hardly any suffering or tragedy is omitted as a consequence of the people's betrayal. Here, as in all other biblical passages quoted, God does not promise an act of grace. All God does, through the

* Nahmanides, in his commentary to the Bible, comments in regard to this verse that God in this declaration impressed upon the people that the fate of life and death rested with them, and he counseled them to choose life.

mouth of his prophets (in Deuteronomy it is Moses), is to announce the alternatives and their results and what man can do in order to choose the one or the other.

The biblical and post-biblical position is that man's will is free and that God does not make him either good or bad. Maimonides, in his classic codification of Jewish law, has summed up the point in the following way:

Free will is bestowed on every human being. If one desires to turn toward the good way and the righteous, he has the power to do so. If one wishes to turn toward the evil way or be wicked, he is at liberty to do so. . . . Let not the notion expressed by foolish Gentiles and most of senseless folk among Israelites pass through your mind that at the beginning of a person's existence, the Almighty decrees that he is to be either righteous or wicked; this is not so: every human being may become righteous like Moses, our teacher, or wicked like Jeroboam; wise or foolish, merciful or cruel; niggardly or generous; and so with all other qualities. There is no one that coerces him or decrees what he is to do or draws him to either of the two ways; but every person turns to the ways which he desires, spontaneously and of his own volition.*

The notion of man's free will could not be expressed more clearly or definitely. Yet there is room for speculation whether the doctrine of free will, as Maimonides presents it, is as commonly accepted as his statement would make one think. In the Bible man is not always offered an alternative and a choice. Thus God says to Moses shortly before his

* In *Mishneh Torah,* "The Laws of Repentance," translated by M. Hyamson (Jerusalem, 1912), 87a.

death: "Behold, you are about to sleep with your fathers; then this people will rise and play the harlot after the strange gods of the land, where they go to be among them, and they will forsake me and break my covenant which I have made with them" (Deut. 31:16). Here God announces as a fact what the Hebrew will do; hence it is already decided, and they no longer have the choice. Yet we have already seen, in the story of the liberation from Egypt, that the statement "God hardened Pharaoh's heart" did not mean that God *wanted* it to harden, but that he did not interfere with the natural process which made it *necessary* for Pharaoh's heart to harden. It seems to follow, then, that in many instances man has freedom of choice, while in some, such as the ones mentioned, man has already gone too far and has lost this freedom. Later Judaism, however, answers this question by clearly distinguishing between foreknowledge and predestination, or even determinism. This is expressed in R. Ismael's saying: "Everything is foreseen, yet freedom of choice is given" (Pirkei Avot,III,19).

The idea that man is free to choose between good and evil and yet may lose this capacity of choice is expressed in the prophetic writings. The prophets consider it their main task to show the people the alternatives and their consequences, and, furthermore, to exercise all their persuasion and moral influence to help people to make their choice. Yet sometimes they "prophesy" disaster because they see that man has lost the freedom of choice. They share the view that man can lose himself to the point of no return. Thus, while usually they announce alternatives, in a number of instances they have predicted unalterable disaster.*

* Cf. the discussion of alternativism and determinism in E. Fromm, *The Heart of Man.*

The idea of man's choice between alternatives in which God does not interfere is continued in the post-biblical tradition. Here the terms *yetzer tov* and *yetzer ha-ra* (good and evil strivings, respectively) are frequently used. A small number of people are free of the evil striving; hence, they have actually lost the freedom to sin; they are the perfect, righteous ones. There is a minority in whom the evil striving dominates; hence, they have lost the possibility to choose. But the majority of us are *benonim*—"in the middle"— in whom both inclinations are balanced, and who therefore can choose between good and evil.

Maimonides, in the following statement, which sums up the Talmudic position, seems also to express the idea that man can lose his freedom of choice, thus contradicting his more generalized philosophical statement.

Every human being has merits and iniquities. One whose merits exceed his iniquities is righteous. He whose iniquities exceed his merits is wicked. If the two balance in an individual, he belongs to the intermediate class. II. So it is with a country. If the merits of all its inhabitants exceed their iniquities, the country is righteous. If their iniquities preponderate, it is a wicked country. So, too, is it with regard to the whole of the world.

2. III. A person whose iniquities exceed his merits perishes forthwith in his wickedness, as it is said, "For the multitude of thy iniquity" (Hosea 9:7). So, too, a country, the iniquities of whose inhabitants preponderate, perishes forthwith, as it is said, "The cry of Sodom and Gomorrah, because it is great" (Gen. 18:20). So, with the entire world, if the iniquities of its human population exceed their merits, they are destroyed forthwith, as it is

said, "And the Lord saw that the wickedness of man was great in the earth" (Gen. 6:5).

IV. This valuation takes into account not the number but the magnitude of merits and iniquities. There may be a single merit that outweighs many iniquities, as it is said, "Because in him there is found some good thing" (I Kings 14:13). And there may be one iniquity that counterbalances many merits, as it is said, "But one sinner [that is, sin] destroyeth much good" (Eccles. 9:19). The valuation is according to the knowledge of the Omniscient God. He alone knows how to set off merit against iniquities.*

It is worth noting that Maimonides, in the prophetic and Talmudic tradition, extends the moral concept from the individual to countries, and eventually to the whole world.

The concept that the existence of the whole world depends on the presence of at least a nucleus of good men is also expressed in the following Talmudic statement: "Abaye said: The world must contain not less than thirty-six righteous men in each generation." Raba said the number of righteous men would have to be 18,000 (Sanhedrin 97b).†

* Maimonides, *Mishneh Torah*, *op. cit.*, 83b–84a.

† The Talmud tries to bridge the opposing views by saying: "There is no difficulty. The former number [36] refers to those who enter [within the barriers, who contemplate the Shekinah] with permission; the latter to those who may enter without permission" (Sanhedrin 97b). This last statement could have served as a model for Kafka's story in *The Trial* of the man who waits before the Law and does not dare to enter because the doorkeeper refuses him permission. The Talmudic statement stresses the point that underlies Kafka's story: man can and should enter the door, even though permission is refused. I do not know, of course, whether the Talmudic passage was known to Kafka.

The attitude of the post-biblical tradition is perhaps best expressed by the idea of the "ten days of repentance" between New Year's Day and the Day of Atonement. During these days man has the opportunity to become aware of his sins, to repent of them, and to change the course of his fate. As the text of the liturgy of the Day of Atonement expresses it: all is decided, the fate of man is determined; *but repentance, prayer, and good deeds avert the severity of the decree.* In other words, man's fate is determined by his previous action—yet he can overcome the determination by a change within himself.

This leads us to a discussion of two central concepts—that of sin and that of repentance. As to the words which are mainly used in the Old Testament for sin, the most important term for "to sin" is *hata.* The root of this word in biblical Hebrew is "to miss" (a goal or the road; for instance, Prov. 19:2, "He who makes haste with his feet *misses*"). It has been used mainly, however, in biblical and later Hebrew in the sense of "sin." The meaning here is quite clear: to sin is to miss (the road). Another biblical word for sin, *avon,* meaning "iniquity," "guilt," or "punishment" (although not precisely "sin" as a generic term), has a root which means "to err" (from the road).* Here only the noun is used, but no longer in the sense of erring—only as iniquity. A third term for sin is *pesha,* usually translated as "transgression," used in the sense of rebellion.†

The word *hata* is the most important and the most frequently used term for sin (especially in a generic sense); its

---

* Cf. N. Gesenius, *Lexicon.*

† Cf. Otto J. Baab, *The Theology of the Old Testament* (New York: Abingdon-Cokesbury Press, 1959), p. 86.

meaning, "to miss" (the road), is highly significant for the biblical as well as for the later Jewish concept of sin. It is more than ignorance or error, more than erroneous *thought;* it is wrong action, the will applied to a wrong aim. Yet to sin is human, almost unavoidable, nothing to be depressed by. As was mentioned before, the Hebrew Bible shows this very clearly by describing all its heroes as sinners, including the greatest figure of all—Moses.*

The meaning of sin as missing the right road corresponds to the term for repent, which is *shuv,* meaning "to return." While the verb is used in this sense in the writing of Hosea (3:5;6:1;7:10), Jeremiah (3:7,12,14,22), Amos (4:6, 8–11) and other prophetic writings, the noun *teshuvah* ("return") is not used in the meaning of repentance in the Bible but only in the later Jewish tradition. A man who repents is a man who "returns." He returns to the right way, to God, to himself. Just as sinning is not an indication of corruption, nor a reason for sadness or guilty submission, *teshuvah* ("repentance") is not the attitude of the meek sinner, accusing himself for his transgressions and prostrating himself. There is no need for contrition or self-accusation; there is little of a sadistic superego or of a masochistic ego in the Jewish concept of sin and repentance. This phenomenon can hardly be understood without reference to a thought which we have already mentioned: man is free and independent. He is even independent from God. Hence his sin is *his* sin, his return is *his* return, and there is no reason

* Jewish commentators of the Bible have interpreted *hata* to mean inadvertent transgression; *avon* as sin committed wtih premeditation; and *pesha* as sin committed in the spirit of rebellion. Cf. commentaries on Ex. 34:7.

for self-accusatory submission. Ezekiel has expressed the principle beautifully: "Have I any pleasure at all that the wicked should die? says the Lord God, and not rather that he should return from his ways and live?" (18:23)

The view the Talmudic tradition takes of the repentant sinner is indicated in the term used for him: *baal teshuvah,* which means literally "the master of return." The term master, which is always used in connection with accomplishment, strength, competence, hardly fits the picture of the meek, contrite, repentant sinner. The "master of return" is the man not ashamed of having sinned and proud of the accomplishment of having returned.* Indicative of the same attitude is the Talmudic saying of R. Abahu, "The place of the 'masters of return' [repentant sinners] cannot be attained even by the completely righteous" (Sanhedrin 99a). That is to say, no man stands higher than the one who took the wrong way and then returned; not even the angels stand higher, according to another Talmudic saying.

We find in the Bible, and still more so in the Talmudic tradition, a marked emphasis on forgiveness, mercy, and on man's capacity to "return." One of the key verses in this respect is God's self-revelation to Moses in Exodus: "The Lord passed before him, and proclaimed, 'The Lord, the Lord, a God merciful and gracious, slow to anger, and abounding in steadfast love and faithfulness, keeping steadfast love for thousands,† forgiving iniquity and transgression and sin, but who will by no means clear the guilty, visiting the iniquity of the fathers upon the children and the chil-

---

* Maimonides in his definition of repentance, characteristically does not mention contrition or shame as parts of repentance.

† Rashi comments that this means at least two thousand generations.

dren's children, to the third and the fourth generation.' " *
While God threatens punishment to the third and fourth
generation, love and compassion are promised to the thousands of generations, and thus God's compassion far outweighs his sense of punishment. But even this punishment of
children for the sins of their fathers is denied in another
verse of the Bible, which says that "The fathers shall not be
put to death for the children, nor shall the children be put
to death for the fathers" (Deut. 24:16).† In the prophetic
writings God's love and compassion for sinning man is
expressed abundantly, as already emphasized. I want to quote
here only one statement which, perhaps as much as any other,
expresses God's compassion: "I was ready to be found by
those who did not seek me" (Is. 65:1).

The rabbinical literature has continued this trend of
thought and has heightened its emphasis. Of many references I shall mention only a few: "[When a man has sinned]
if he has great advocates he is saved, but if not he is not
saved. And these are man's advocates: repentance [*teshuvah*]

* To this translation some comments seem to be in order: the
Hebrew *rahum*, which is here translated as "steadfast love," is usually
translated as "merciful" and means "soft," "gentle," "wide,"
"womb," in other Semitic languages (cf. Gesenius, *Lexicon*). In
Hebrew the noun *rehem* means "womb." The noun (plural)
rahamim is by many supposed to be the plural of *rehem* = "womb,"
and hence to mean "brotherly feeling of those born from the same
womb" or "motherly feeling." The traditional translation, "mercy,"
does not do justice to the essential meaning of the Hebrew word.
Compassion is more adequate; (motherly) love seems to be the nearest
to the original meaning. The same holds true for the adjective *rahum*,
which is used with reference to God in the verse quoted above. The
translation "compassionate" or "loving" seems to me the most adequate.

† Cf. also Ezekiel 18:2–9.

and good deeds. And even if 999 argue for his guilt, while one argues in his favor he is saved" (Shabbat 32a). Or: "Whoever does something [wrong] and repents of it he is forgiven at once" (Hagiga 5a). The idea of God's forgiveness is also expressed in the view that God has two thrones: one for justice and one for compassion (Sanhedrin 38b).*

There are some other aspects of the Jewish concepts of repentance which are worth mentioning. "Return" is an independent act of man, not a passive submission. In a Talmudic story this idea is shown with some humor:

It was said of R. Eleazar b. Dordai that once, on hearing that there was a certain harlot in one of the towns by the sea who accepted a purse of *denarii* for her hire, he took a purse of *denarii* and crossed seven rivers for her sake. As he was with her, she broke wind and said: As this blown wind will not return from where it came, so will Eleazar b. Dordai never be received in repentance. He thereupon went, sat between two hills and mountains and exclaimed: O, ye hills and mountains, plead for mercy for me! They replied: How shall we pray for thee? We stand in need of it ourselves, for it is said, *For the mountains shall depart and the hills be removed* (Is. 54: 10). So he exclaimed: Heaven and earth, plead ye for mercy for me! They, too, replied: How shall we pray for thee? We stand in need of it ourselves, for it is said, *For*

* It is interesting to note that the rabbinic tradition is well aware of the differences in the use of YHWH (The Lord) and *Elohim* (God). While modern critics of the Scriptures have used this difference as the key to discover two basic literary sources of the Bible, the rabbinical view has made this intrepretation: YHWH denotes God under his attribute of compassion; *Elohim* under the attribute of justice.

the heavens shall vanish away like smoke, and the earth shall wax old like a garment (Is. 51:6). He then exclaimed: Sun and moon, plead ye for mercy for me! But they also replied: How shall we pray for thee? We stand in need of it ourselves, for it is said, *Then the moon shall be confounded and the sun ashamed* (Is. 24:23). He exclaimed: Ye stars and constellations, plead ye for mercy for me! Said they: How shall we pray for thee? We stand in need of it ourselves, for it is said, *And all the hosts of heaven shall moulder away* (Is. 34:4). Said he: The matter then depends upon me alone! Having placed his head between his knees, he wept aloud until his soul departed. Then a *bat-kol* [heavenly voice] was heard proclaiming: "R. Eleazar b. Dordai is destined for the life of the world to come!" *

Avodah Zara 17a–b

Another aspect of "return" which is related to the mood of inner activity is the absence of sadness or depression in connection with repentance. The Day of Atonement, for instance, while it is a day of fasting, is in no way a day of sadness which could be produced by a harsh and accusing "super-ego." Anyone who has witnessed the traditional celebration of this day will confirm that it is a day of utter seriousness and self-examination, but filled with a mood of joy, rather than sadness. This corresponds to a principle running through the Jewish tradition which, briefly formulated, says:

* The central issue of this story, aside from the emphasis on God's forgiveness as a result of repentance, is the sentence, "The matter then depends upon me alone!" If man wants to "return," nobody else can help him. He must first be able to be all by himself and to rely on nobody except himself. In other words: return requires independence as a condition. It is not surrender; it is the expression of freedom.

sadness is bad—joy is good. It is often believed that this principle of joy was emphasized only by the Hasidic movement, whose motto was the verse of Psalms: "Serve the Lord in joy." But this emphasis on joy is by no means only a Hasidic peculiarity. There is perhaps no better indication for this than the sentence in Deuteronomy (28:47), to which reference was made before, where the main guilt of the Hebrews is summarized: "[You have sinned] Because you did not serve the Lord your God with joyfulness and gladness of heart, by reason of the abundance of all things."

The same idea is also expressed in a Talmudic saying: "This teaches you that the Divine Presence rests [upon man] neither through gloom, nor through sloth, nor through frivolity, nor through levity, nor through talk, nor through idle chatter, but only through a matter of joy (Shabbat 30b).*

A Hasidic master (Shmelke of Nikolsburg) interpreted this Talmudic saying to mean: "But you must know that the weeping on this day [of Atonement] will not avail if there is sadness in it." †

There are many more Hasidic utterances directed against falling into a mood of sadness while contemplating one's sins. A very characteristic one is the following:

> Whoever talks about and reflects upon an evil thing he has done is thinking of the vileness he has perpetrated, and what one thinks, therein is one caught—with one's whole soul one is caught utterly in what one thinks, and so he is still caught in vileness. And he will surely not be able to

---

* It must be also taken into account that the Sabbath is a day of joy in which all mourning is interrupted.

† Quoted by S. Y. Agnon, *Days of Awe* (New York: Schocken Books, 1948), p. 207.

turn, for his spirit will coarsen and his heart rot, and besides this, a sad mood may come upon him. What would you? Stir filth this way or that, and it is still filth. To have sinned or not to have sinned—what does it profit us in heaven? In the time I am brooding on this, I could be stringing pearls for the joy of heaven. That is why it is written: "Depart from evil, and do good"—turn wholly from evil, do not brood in its way, and do good. You have done wrong? Then balance it by doing right.*

We find a similar spirit in the following Hasidic story: "Said the Kobriner: 'In Psalm 9:3, we read: "Thou turnest man to dejection and sayest: Repent, ye children of men." But I say, "O Lord, if Thou turnest man to dejection, how can you expect him to repent? Grant him his necessities, and his heart will be free to turn to Thee.' " (The Kobriner makes use of a paraphrase here, translating the Hebrew *dakha* to read "dejection" rather than "contrition.") †

In order to understand this attitude toward sin and repentance fully we must remember that in the Jewish tradition sin and evil "imaginings" are part of every man (with the exception of those exceptional ones who have never been tempted). This idea is not one of "collective guilt" or of "original sin," but is based on the humanist concept that we all share in the same human nature, hence *"we* have sinned, stolen, robbed, murdered," and so on, as it is said in the service of the Day of Atonement. Because we all share in the same humanity, there is nothing inhuman in sinning, hence

* Isaac Meir of Ger; quoted in *Time and Eternity,* edited by N. N. Glatzer (New York: Schocken Books, 1946).

† M. S. Kleinman, Hebrew, *Or Yesharim* (Piotrkov, 1924), p. 105; quoted by L. Newman, p. 380.

nothing to be ashamed of, or to be despised for. Our inclination to sin is as human as our inclination to do good and as our capacity to "return." *

Having discussed in the previous pages the biblical and post-biblical emphasis on compassion and "return" rather than on threat, it seems advisable to discuss the distinction between two concepts which are often confused: "threat" and "prediction." Two examples may help to illustrate the problem. An example of a threat would be an employer who tells his worker: "If you do not work fourteen hours a day and accomplish such and such an amount of work, I shall fire you." An example of a prediction would be that of a man telling another: "If you touch this high-voltage wire you will die." In one sense the two cases are similar: a person is warned to do (or not to do) a certain thing, and he is warned that if he acts against the warning, severe consequences will follow.

The difference is also clear. In the first case the threatening

---

* Cf. the following statement by Master Eckhart on sin, which resembles in certain aspects the Talmudic position: "But if a man rises completely above sin and turns away from it absolutely, then God, who is faithful, acts as if the sinner had never fallen into sin. He will not allow him to suffer one moment for all his sins. Even if there were as many of them as all men had ever committed, God will never make him atone for them. With this man he may have all the intimacy that he ever achieved with a creature. If he should really find him ready now, he will not consider what the man had been before. God is a God of the present. He takes you and receives you just as he finds you, not as the person you were, but as what you are. God will gladly suffer, and has suffered for years, all the wrongs and dishonor that might come to him as a result of all the sins of the world, in order that man may afterward arrive at a full recognition of his love and in order that his love and gratitude may be all the greater and his zeal the more ardent, which quite often and rightly happens after sin."

person uses the threat to force the other to give in to his will. In the second case the "threatening" person states a sequence of cause and effect which is independent of his will; furthermore, his threat does not have the function of serving himself. It is, in fact, not a threat but a prediction of cause and effect. The prediction becomes true, not due to an action on the part of the one who makes it but through circumstances beyond his will, power, or interest. Quite obviously it is not always easy to distinguish clearly between a threat and a prediction. Does a father, telling his son that he will spank him if he does not do his homework, threaten him or is his threat an indirect expression of the prediction that he will fail in school (and in life) if he does not acquire self-discipline and a sense of responsibility? The distinction is all the more difficult to make since often the threatener will hide his personal interest behind the façade of a seemingly objective prediction. The distinction becomes even more difficult if, on the contrary, an objectively valid prediction is expressed as if it were the threat of an irrational and exploitative authority. The latter difficulty arises often in the biblical stories. When we read that God threatens a particular punishment if the Hebrews do not obey a certain command, we seem to be dealing with the threat of an irrational authority insisting that his will be done. However, if we look more closely at the alternatives between life and death, blessing and curse, then we will discover that Moses and the prophets are usually announcing nothing but the alternatives of the moral law. Whether this law is expressed in terms of God's commandments and the ensuing punishment or in term of a psychologist's prediction that certain attitudes and actions will result in certain results, the essential character of a prognosis remains the same. In order to decide what is a threat or what is a prediction, it is necessary to examine the validity of the alternative proposed, and, furthermore, whether the predicted consequences are true.

Those who do not believe in a moral law and its realistic long-range consequences will, of course, never agree that the kind of alternative as announced by the Bible is a realistic alternative and not just a threat. Those, on the other hand, including myself, who are convinced that there are moral laws which have their inescapable consequences for man will examine the biblical alternatives as to their validity.

Nevertheless, inasmuch as the Old Testament in many of its parts speaks in a very authoritarian spirit, even its predictions often sound like threats, and in many cases they are. I do not want to imply that all biblical threats are nothing but predictions; I want to stress the difference, in principle, between threat and prediction, and to emphasize that many biblical "threats" are really predictions. To decide where this is the case and where it is not would go beyond the scope of this chapter.

vi *The Way:*
HALAKHAH

I have indicated that the main emphasis of biblical and later Jewish religious thought is not on knowledge *about* God but on the imitation of God. This imitation is to be attempted by following the right way of living, which is called *halakhah*. The word has its root in the word "to walk." *Halakhah* means, then, the way in which one walks; this way leads to an ever increasing approximation of God's actions.

Before discussing the details of the Way, I want to indicate briefly the principles underlying the *halakhah*. The description of these principles need not, in fact, be more than a summary of those that have already been discussed in the chapters on the concepts of God, man, and history.

In the biblical and later Jewish tradition there are a number of central values: the affirmation of life, love, justice, freedom, and truth. These values are not disparate items, independent from each other, but form a value syndrome.

The biblical story of creation gives a striking and poetic expression to the affirmative attitude toward life. After creating light, "God saw that the light was good" (Gen. 1:4). After creating the land and the sea, "God saw that it was good" (Gen. 1:10). After creating the vegetation, "God saw that it was good" (Gen. 1:12). After creating day and night, "God saw that it was good" (Gen. 1:18). After creating the first fish and the first birds, "God saw that is was good. And God blessed them, saying, 'Be fruitful and multiply and fill the waters in the seas, and let birds multiply on the earth' " (Gen. 1:21–22). After God had created the animals on the earth, "God saw that it was good" (Gen. 1:25). After all creation had been finished, "God saw everything that he had made, and behold, it was very* good" (Gen. 1:31). Only when God had created man did he not say, "It is good." According to a Hasidic story, God did not say that it was good, because man was created as an open system, meant to grow and to develop, and was not finished, as the rest of creation had been.

Man must choose between the basic alternatives of life and death. In the verse, "See, I have set before you this day life and good, death and evil" (Deut. 30:15), life is equated with good, and death with evil, and some verses later the choice is formulated "that I have set before you life and

* The commentary of Sforno says that the "very" is added to denote that the perfection of the total creation exceeds that of its separate parts.

death, blessing and curse; therefore choose life, that you
and your descendants may live" (Deut. 30:19).

Life is the highest norm for man; God is alive and man is
alive; the fundamental choice for man is that between growth
and decay.

One might ask how man can make a choice between life
and death; man is either alive or dead, and there is no choice,
except if one were to consider the possibility of suicide. But
what the biblical text refers to is not life and death as biological facts but as principles and values. To be alive is to
grow, to develop, to respond; to be dead (even if one is
alive biologically) means to stop growing, to fossilize, to
become a thing. Many people never face the clear alternative
between the values of life and those of death, and hence they
live in neither world or they become "zombies," their bodies
being alive and their souls dead. To choose life is the
necessary condition for love, freedom, and truth. It is also
the condition for loving God, for "not those who are dead
praise you," as the Psalmist says.

Albert Schweitzer's principle, "reverence for life," is also
characteristic of the later thinking in the Jewish tradition.
I want to mention only one striking example. All commandments, be it the keeping of the Sabbath, the food rituals,
prayer, or the like, the observance of which is a strict duty
according to the Talmudic system, are suspended when their
observance might endanger life. Not only is it permissible to
break these laws under such circumstances, but it is one's
duty to break the law in order to save life.*

However, if an alien power should try to compel a Jew,
either publicly or privately, under pain of death to blas-

---

* See also Yoma 85b: "He shall live by them [the commandments,
cf. Leviticus 18:5] but not die because of them."

pheme God, to shed blood, or to commit incest, the individual should suffer death rather than comply. If the authority should order a Jew publicly to break even a minor commandment, the intention of such an order being the destruction of Judaism, he should suffer death. But while this is the law, as codified by Maimonides in the *Mishneh Torah,* a number of outstanding Talmudic sages disagreed, and in practice accepted the command of the Romans to desist from teaching and from ordination.

Closely related to the principle of affirmation of life is that of love. The best-known and most general command to love is that expressed in Leviticus (19:18): "You shall love your neighbor as yourself." No lesser a man than R. Akiba described this command as the fundamental law of the Torah, and the great Hillel, when asked by a pagan to explain to him the Torah in the time in which he could stand on one foot said, "Do not do unto others what you would not want to be done unto you. This is the essence, and the rest is commentary; go and learn" (Shabbat 31a).

There is some doubt as to whether the command in Leviticus to love your neighbor refers to the member of the same religion or nationality (in this case other Hebrews) or whether it refers to any other person, to any human being. Some Old Testament scholars have claimed that the word *rea* (translated as "neighbor") refers only to a fellow national; others have claimed that it refers to any other human being.* Considering all the arguments pro and con, it seems to me difficult to arrive at a definite decision, since

* Hermann Cohen especially has tried with great ingenuity and scholarship to prove the latter. Cf. H. Cohen, *Jüdische Schriften I* (Berlin: C. A. Schwetschke & Sohn, 1924), pp. 145–195, and his *Religion der Vernunft,* pp. 137 ff.

the word *rea* is used in the sense of "friend," "fellow citizen," as well as just "another" with whom one stands in any reciprocal relation.* The sentence could be translated, then, as referring to another human being as well as to fellow citizens. However, the fact that the sentence says in its first part: "You shall not take vengeance, or bear any grudge against the sons of your own people" and then continues, "but you shall love your neighbor as yourself," seems, in my opinion, to speak somewhat more in favor of the interpretation "as fellow citizens."

But whatever the meaning of *rea* is in this command, there is no doubt that the Bible commands love for the "stranger," that is, for him who is powerless because he does not share the same blood or the same religion. Leviticus 19:33–34 says: "When a stranger sojourns with you in your land, you shall not do him wrong. The stranger who sojourns with you shall be to you as the native among you, and you shall love him as yourself; for you were strangers in the land of Egypt: I am the Lord your God." It has been claimed that the term "stranger" (*ger*) used here refers to one who has been converted to the Jewish religion. While the word can be used in this sense, it is evident, as Cohen has already pointed out, that it does not have this meaning here. By explaining the command regarding the love of the stranger by the fact that the Hebrews were "strangers" in Egypt, the text makes it perfectly clear that the *ger* is here the stranger who does not participate in the same religion and who is not in any sense a convert. (The term *ger* means, in general, "sojourner," "temporary dweller.") †

The same reference to the Hebrews' role as strangers is

* Cf. Gesenius, *Lexicon.*
† *Ibid.*

made in Deuteronomy (10:19): "Love the stranger [so-
journer] therefore; for you were strangers in the land of
Egypt." In another verse a further reference is made to the
Hebrews' past as strangers in Egypt: "You shall not oppress
a stranger; you know the heart of a stranger, for you were
strangers in the land of Egypt" (Ex. 23:9). In this verse we
find not only the reference to the Hebrews' sojourn in Egypt
but a very significant explanation of the reason for not
oppressing (or, as in the other verses, for loving) the
stranger: you know the heart of the stranger, because you
yourselves were strangers in Egypt. The principle is that
the love for the stranger as another human being, as one who
is nothing other than human (precisely because he does not
share my blood, customs, religion), is rooted in one's knowledge of him—and this knowledge is based on the commonly
shared experience of being a stranger, oppressed and suffering. In a broader sense the verse says: All love is based on
knowledge of the other; all knowledge of the other is based
on shared experience. I cannot understand in another that
which I do not experience in myself; and to be human
means that we carry within ourselves all of humanity—hence
all of the stranger. As long as I have not discovered the
stranger as being human, I know myself only as the social
being who is like all those with whom he shares the same
customs and language. In this case I know myself only as
the "social man." Only by "knowing the heart of the
stranger" do I see behind the social screen that masks me
from myself as a human being, do I know myself as the
"universal man." Once I have discovered the stranger within
myself I cannot hate the stranger outside of myself, because
he has ceased to be a stranger to me. The command "love
thy enemy" is implied already in the Old Testament com-

mand: "love the stranger." If the stranger is the stranger within me, the enemy is also the enemy within me; he ceases to be the enemy, because he is I.*

The "stranger" appears in still another dimension in the Hebrew Bible, not only as the unknown human being, but as the *powerless* human being. Thus, for instance, we find the command: "When you reap your harvest in your field, and have forgotten a sheaf in the field, you shall not go back to get it; it shall be for the stranger [sojourner], the fatherless, and the widow; that the Lord your God may bless you in all the work of your hands" (Deut. 24:19). Here, as in many other passages of the Pentateuch and Prophets, the main principle of social justice is expounded: to protect those who have no power (the widow, the orphan, the poor, and the stranger) against those who have power.

Biblical ethics are not primarily concerned with wealth and poverty as such but with the social relations between those that are powerful and those that are powerless. The stranger, being a symbol of the person without power, therefore deserves special protection from the standpoint of the law, as well as from that of morality.

Man's love and God's love in biblical and later Jewish thought are inseparable; if man is to be like God, God's love must be the example for man. God appears in the Bible as the God of justice and the God of compassion. While in some older parts of the Bible the emphasis is on the God of justice more than on the God of compassion, in the prophetic literature the concept of God's love and compas-

---

* As we have already seen, the concept of the stranger finds its more radical expression in the prophetic ideas regarding the unity of all nations in the messianic time, in the concept of the Noachites, and the "pious among the Gentiles," in the later Jewish tradition.

sion abounds. Nothing could express the spirit of God's love better than the short sentences in Isaiah: "I was ready to be sought by those who did not ask for me; I was ready to be found by those who did not seek me. I said, 'Here am I, here am I,' to a nation that did not call on my name" (65:1); or: "For a brief moment I forsook you, but with great compassion I will gather you" (54:7).

Of the many descriptions of God's love found in the Prophets I want to mention only one more: Hosea's analogy between Israel and a wife having become a harlot. Yet in spite of that, the husband does not stop loving the wife and "in that day . . . I will betroth you to me for ever; I will bethroth you to me in righteousness and in justice, in steadfast love, and in mercy. I will betroth you to me in faithfulness; and you shall know the Lord" (Hosea 2:19–20).

God's love for man finds many expressions in the Talmudic literature. Thus one Talmudic story characteristically expresses this spirit: "R. Ishmael b. Elisha says, I once entered into the innermost part [of the sanctuary] to offer incense and saw Akatriel Yah [lit., crown of God], the Lord of Hosts, seated upon a high and exalted throne. He said to me: Ishmael, my son, Bless me! I replied, may it be thy will that thy mercy may suppress thy anger and thy mercy prevail over thy other attributes, so that thou mayest deal with thy children according to the attribute of mercy, and mayest, in their behalf, stop short of the limit of strict justice. And he nodded to me with his head. Here we learn that the blessing of an ordinary man must not be considered lightly in your eyes" (Berakhot 7a).

In both the Old Testament and the later Jewish tradition love is inseparably related to the value of freedom and independence. We have seen that for man to be fully born, that is, to become fully human, he must cut the umbilical cord—that which connects him with his mother as well as that which connects him with his family and his soil. But the cutting of his incestuous ties* is not enough. Man cannot be fully human if he is not free from man. It is precisely because of the central role of freedom in the value system of the Bible that the liberation from Egypt is the central event in the Jewish tradition. It is worth noting that the religious constitution of Israel, the law given at Mount Sinai, is preceded by the social revolution, for only free men, not slaves, can receive the Torah. God could reveal himself to Abraham and to Moses as individuals, but Israel can become a "holy" people only as the result of the liberation from Egypt. Easter, which had been the feast of the awakening of nature in many other cults, was transformed into the day of revolution by the Bible.

In the later Jewish tradition the idea of freedom is expressed in many ways. The Mishnah says, with regard to the biblical sentence, that the writing of God was "graven" upon the tables of the law: " 'And the tables were the work of God, and the writing was the writing of God, graven upon the tables' (Ex. 32:16). Read not *harut* (graven) but *herut* (freedom), for no man is free for thee but he that occupies himself with the study of the Torah" (Avot VI).

Stating that Judaism is not centered around right belief but around right action does not mean that the Bible and the later tradition are not related to the concept of God. But it does mean that in the Jewish tradition the existence of the one God is the premise for the practice of the Way. The task of man is to live and to act in the right manner, and thus

* Cf. the discussion on incest as referring not to a sexual, but to a deep emotional, tie in E. Fromm, *The Heart of Man.*

to become like God. What matters from the standpoint of the Jewish tradition is whether a man fulfills the law, not what his views about God are.

The nature of the Jewish law is very evident in the meaning of the word *torah,* which signifies "direction," "instruction," and "law." *The Torah is a law which directs man to imitate God by instructing him in the right action.*

The most fundamental biblical formulation of the law is to be found in the Ten Commandments, which are written in two versions (Ex. 20:2–14 and Deut. 5:6–18). Both are very similar, the main difference being in the commandment dealing with the observation of the Sabbath, which is given in Exodus with reference to God's rest after the creation of the world, and in Deuteronomy with reference to the liberation of the Hebrews from Egyptian bondage.

Here follows the text from Exodus:

"I am the Lord your God, who brought you out of the land of Egypt, out of the house of bondage.

"You shall have no other gods before me.

"You shall not make for yourself a graven image, or any likeness of anything that is in heaven above, or that is in the earth beneath, or that is in the water under the earth; you shall not bow down to them or serve them; for I the Lord your God am a jealous God, visiting the iniquity of the fathers upon the children to the third and the fourth generation of those who hate me, but showing steadfast love to thousands of those who love me and keep my commandments.

"You shall not take the name of the Lord your God in vain; for the Lord will not hold him guiltless who takes his name in vain.

"Remember the sabbath day, to keep it holy. Six days you shall labor, and do all your work; but the seventh day is a sabbath to the Lord your God; in it you shall not do any work, you, or your son, or your daughter, your manservant, or your maidservant, or your cattle, or the sojourner who is within your gates; for in six days the Lord made heaven and earth, the sea, and all that is in them, and rested the seventh day; therefore the Lord blessed the sabbath day and hallowed it.

"Honor your father and your mother, that your days may be long in the land which the Lord your God gives you.

"You shall not kill.

"You shall not commit adultery.

"You shall not steal.

"You shall not bear false witness against your neighbor.

"You shall not covet your neighbor's house; you shall not covet your neighbor's wife, or his manservant, or his maidservant, or his ox, or his ass, or anything that is your neighbor's."

The Ten Commandments can easily be grouped into the following categories:

1) About God: here we find the proclamation of God as the God of liberation, the prohibition of idolatry and of the empty use of God's name; there is no commandment to love God or to have faith in him, but only the statement that God *is* and that he is the liberator of the people.

2) The commandment regarding the Sabbath.

3) The commandment to honor one's parents: to *honor*, not to fear or to *love* them.

4) The prohibition regarding murder, adultery, stealing,*
bearing false witness, and coveting one's neighbor's posses-
sions. All the prohibitions in this fourth part are essentially
directed against greed, envy, and hate of one's fellow man.
There is no ritual command or prohibition in the Ten
Commandments. Besides those which are social in nature
(like honoring one's parents and the prohibition of aggression against one's neighbor) are the religious command not
to worship idols and the command to observe the Sabbath.†

The post-biblical tradition has enlarged and developed
the biblical law. It created a system of *halakhah,* which
covers every aspect of man's activities. According to Maimonides, who systematized the whole post-biblical law in his
classic *Mishneh Torah,* the *halakhah* can be divided into the
the following classes: ‡

1) Laws which form fundamental principles, including
repentance and fasting.

2) Laws dealing with the prohibition of idolatry.

3) Laws connected with the improvement of the moral
conditions of mankind.

4) Laws relating to charity, loans, gifts, and so on.

---

* One Talmudic opinion interprets stealing here as referring only
to the stealing of people, not to the stealing of things.

† It is interesting to note that, in essence, the Ten Commandments
do not differ greatly from the seven Noachite commandments. If we
do not count the first sentence as a commandment (according to one
school of thought in the Talmud), there remains essentially the prohibition of idolatry and the commandments forbidding aggression
against one's neighbor. The commandment to honor one's parents is
not too different from the social order which we find in the Noachite
commandments, for every social order is based on a certain respect
for tradition. The only new commandment is that referring to the Sabbath.

‡ Cf. Maimonides, *Guide for the Perplexed,* pp. 329 ff.

5) Laws relating to the prevention of wrong and violence.

6) Laws on theft, robbery, false witness, and the like.

7) Laws regulating business transactions of men with each other.

8) Laws concerning the Sabbath and holy days.

9) Laws concerning religious rites and ceremonies.

10) Laws relating to the Sanctuary (Temple), its vessels, and its ministers.

11) Laws relating to sacrifices.

12) Laws relating to things clean and unclean.

13) Laws relating to forbidden food, and the like.

14) Laws relating to forbidden sexual intercourse.

Maimonides' classification shows that the *halakhah* covers all and every sphere of human activity. This concept of the law is entirely different from the Western concept in which law refers either to crimes or to such interpersonal transactions as contracts, which can be subject to litigation. The *halakhah* tries to fill all human activity with a certain spirit —that of the imitation of God. The practice of the law is true religiosity, the knowledge of the law is the substitute for theology. One rabbinical source lists what it considers the most important laws, and this enumeration gives a picture of the peculiar mixture of various spheres of activities dealt with by the law: "These are the things the fruits of which man enjoys in this world, while the capital remains for him in the world to come: to honor his father and mother, to give charitably, to go to the house of learning early in the morning and in the evening, to grant hospitality to the wanderer, to care for the sick, to provide for a bride, to bury the dead, to make peace between men; but the study of the law is more important than all" (Peah I,1).

Each law is called a *mitzvah*, which means both duty and command. While the Talmud speaks often of the fact that man must accept the "yoke" of the *mitzvot*, by the very nature of the law it is not supposed to be felt and, indeed, I believe, has generally not been felt as a burden but as a meaningful way of living. Clearly, many parts of the law, like the sacrifices, food taboos, laws of ritual cleanliness, have no rational or educational function.* But many other laws direct man to act justly, lovingly, and thus tend to educate and transform him. An example of the development from biblical to post-biblical law in the direction of increasing ethical refinement is the following: the biblical law "you shall not put an obstacle before the blind" is interpreted in a wide, ethical sense as implying that one must not take advantage of any person's helplessness, ignorance, and so forth. It is quite obvious that such a law is of great ethical relevance for the relations between man and man. In the same spirit the prohibition of murder is extended to that of not humiliating another person. The Talmud says: "He who makes his neighbor ashamed in the presence of others is as if he had shed his blood." (The statement is based on a pun: the Hebrew word for shaming is *malbim* [lit., "to make white"] interpreted here as shedding blood; the blood leaves the head and thus the face becomes white.)

The biblical law that a man is to be executed for a crime only if two witnesses have seen him committing it, had been so sharpened by the oral traditions that it practically

---

* In the rabbinical literature they are often considered to be justified only because of the fact that they are God's commands. That they have done much to guarantee the unity and survival of the Jews as a nation can hardly be doubted.

amounted to the abolishment of capital punishment. According to the Talmud, one court that had sentenced a man to death within a period of seventy years was called "a bloody court." Many rabbis have added their personal norms to the *mitzvot* of the Talmud. There were many, for instance, who refused to denounce a thief and to deliver him to the authorities for punishment, or who would give him what he had stolen as a gift, in order not to have him burdened with the (moral or legal) charge of a crime. All such rules and principles were elaborations made on the basic law of loving one's neighbor.

The spirit of the law, as it was developed by the rabbis through the centuries, was one of justice, brotherly love, respect for the individual, and the devotion of life to one's human development. There was no vow of poverty among the rabbis; but to devote oneself to learning was always considered to be the supreme task, not to be interfered with by mundane interests.

Most of the biblical and rabbinical laws are understandable in their ethical and human significance (aside from those which have a pure ritualistic and usually archaic meaning); one law, however, which has a central position within the whole system, has often not been adequately understood, and hence needs a more detailed interpretation: the law concerning the Sabbath.

There can be no doubt of the fact that the Sabbath is a, or perhaps *the*, central institution of biblical and rabbinical religion. It is commanded in the Decalogue; it is one of the few religious laws emphasized by the great reforming Prophets; it has a central place in rabbinical thought, and as long as Judaism exists in its traditional customs, it was and is the most outstanding phenomenon of Jewish religious practice. It is no exaggeration to say that the spiritual and moral survival of the Jews during two thousand years of persecution and humiliation would hardly have been possible without the one day in the week when even the poorest and most wretched Jew was transformed into a man of dignity and pride, when the beggar was changed into a king. But in order not to think that this statement is a crude exaggeration, one must have witnessed the traditional practice of the Sabbath in its authentic form. Whoever thinks that he knows what the Sabbath is because he has seen the candles lit has little idea of the atmosphere the traditional Sabbath creates.

The reason why the Sabbath has so central a place within Jewish law lies in the fact that the Sabbath is the expression of the central idea of Judaism: the idea of freedom; the idea of complete harmony between man and nature, man and man; the idea of the anticipation of the messianic time and of man's defeat of time, sadness, and death.*

The modern mind does not see much of a problem in the Sabbath institution. That man should rest from his work one day every week sounds to us like a self-evident, social-hygienic measure intended to give him the physical and spiritual rest and relaxation he needs in order not to be swallowed up by his daily work, and to enable him to work better during the six working days. No doubt this explanation is true as far as it goes, but it does not answer

* In the following pages I draw upon the ideas and the material of a paper on "The Sabbath Ritual," in E. Fromm, *The Forgotten Language* (New York: Holt, Rinehart and Winston, 1951), pp. 241 ff. In the same year (1951) a book entitled *The Sabbath* was published by Abraham J. Heschel, which contains a beautiful and profound analysis of the Sabbath (New York: Farrar, Straus & Giroux).

some questions that arise if we pay closer attention to the
Sabbath law of the Bible and particularly to the Sabbath
ritual as it developed in the post-biblical tradition.

Why is this social-hygienic law so important that is was
placed among the Ten Commandments, which otherwise
stipulate only the fundamental religious and ethical principles? Why is it explained by equating it with God's rest on
the seventh day, and what does this "rest" mean? Is God
pictured in such anthropomorphic terms as to need a rest
after six days of hard work? Why is the Sabbath explained
in the second version of the Ten Commandments in terms
of freedom rather than in terms of God's rest? What is the
common denominator of the two explanations? Moreover—
and this is perhaps the most important question—how can
we understand the intricacies of the Sabbath ritual in the
light of the social-hygienic interpretation of rest? In the Old
Testament a man who "gathers sticks" (Num. 4:32 ff.) is
considered a violator of the Sabbath law and punished by
death. In the later development, not only work in our modern
sense is forbidden, but activities such as the following:
making any kind of fire, even if it is for the sake of conven-
ience and does not require any physical effort; pulling a
single blade of grass from the soil; carrying anything, even
something as light as a handkerchief, on one's person. All
this is not work in the sense of physical effort; its avoidance
is often more of an inconvenience and discomfort than its
execution would be. Are we dealing here with extravagant
and compulsive exaggerations of an originally "sensible"
ritual, or is our understanding of the ritual perhaps faulty
and in need of revision?

A more detailed analysis of the symbolic meaning of the

Sabbath ritual will show that we are dealing not with obsessive overstrictness but with a concept of work and rest that is different from our modern concept.

To begin with, the concept of work underlying the biblical and later Talmudic concepts is not one of physical effort, but it can be defined thus: *"Work" is any interference by man, be it constructive or destructive, with the physical world. "Rest" is a state of peace between man and nature.* Man must leave nature untouched, not change it in any way, either by building or by destroying anything. Even the smallest change made by man in the natural process is a violation of rest. The Sabbath is the day of complete harmony between man and nature. "Work" is any kind of disturbance of the man-nature equilibrium. On the basis of this general definition, we can understand the Sabbath ritual.

Any heavy work, like plowing or building, is work in this, as well as in our modern, sense. But lighting a match and pulling up a blade of grass, while not requiring any effort, are symbols of human interference with the natural process, are a breach of peace between man and nature. On the basis of this principle, we can understand the Talmudic prohibition of carrying anything, even of little weight, on one's person. In fact, the carrying of something, as such, is not forbidden. I can carry a heavy load within my house or my estate without violating the Sabbath law. But I must not carry even a handkerchief from one domain to another—for instance, from the private domain of the house to the public domain of the street. This law is an extension of the idea of peace from the social to the natural realm. A man must not interfere with or change the natural equilibrium and he must refrain from changing the social equilibrium. That means not only not to do business but also to avoid the most

primitive form of transference of property, namely, its local
transference from one domain to another.

The Sabbath symbolizes a state of union between man
and nature and between man and man. By not working—that
is to say, by not participating in the process of natural and
social change—man is free from the chains of time, although
only for one day a week.

The full significance of this idea can be understood only in
the context of the biblical philosophy of the relationship between man and nature and the concept of the messianic time.
The Sabbath is the anticipation of the messianic time, which
is sometimes called "the time of the perpetual Sabbath"; but
it is not purely the *symbolic* anticipation of the messianic
time—it is its real precursor. As the Talmud puts it, "If all
of Israel observed two Sabbaths [consecutively] fully only
once, the messiah would be here" (Shabbat 118a). The
Sabbath is the anticipation of the messianic time, not through
a magic ritual, but through a form of practice which puts
man in a real situation of harmony and peace. The different
practice of life transforms man. This transformation has been
expressed in the Talmud in the following way: "R. Simeon
b. Lakish said: 'On the eve of the Sabbath, the Holy One
Blessed Be He, gives to man an additional soul, and at the
close of the Sabbath he withdraws it from him'" (Beitzah
16a).

"Rest" in the sense of the traditional Sabbath concept
is quite different from "rest" being defined as not working,
or not making an effort (just as "peace" —*shalom*—in the
prophetic tradition is more than merely the absence of war;
it expresses harmony, wholeness).* On the Sabbath, man

* Cf. E. Fromm, "The Prophetic Concept of Peace," in *The Dogma
of Christ.*

ceases completely to be an animal whose main occupation is to fight for survival and to sustain his biological life. On the Sabbath, man is fully man, with no task other than to be human. In the Jewish tradition it is not work which is a supreme value, but rest, the state that has no other purpose than that of being human.

There is one other aspect of the Sabbath ritual which is relevant to its full understanding. The Sabbath seems to have been an old Babylonian holiday, celebrated every seventh day (*Shapatu*) of a moon month. But its meaning was quite different from that of the biblical Sabbath. The Babylonian *Shapatu* was a day of mourning and self-castigation. It was a somber day, dedicated to the planet Saturn (our "Saturday" is still in its name devoted to Saturn), whose wrath one wanted to placate by self-castigation and self-punishment. But in the Bible, the holy day lost the character of self-castigation and mourning; it is no longer an "evil" day but a good one; the Sabbath becomes the very opposite of the sinister *Shapatu*. It becomes the day of joy and pleasure. Eating, drinking, sexual love, in addition to studying the Scriptures and religious writings, have characterized the Jewish celebration of the Sabbath throughout the last two thousand years. From a day of submission to the evil powers of Saturn, Sabbath has become a day of freedom and joy.

This change in mood and meaning can be fully understood only if we consider the meaning of Saturn. Saturn (in the old astrological and metaphysical tradition) symbolizes time. He is the god of time and hence the god of death. Inasmuch as man is like God, gifted with a soul, with reason, love, and freedom, he is not subject to time or death. But inasmuch as man is an animal with a body subject to the laws of nature, he is a slave to time and death. The Babylonians sought to appease the lord of time by self-castigation. The Bible, in its Sabbath concept, makes an entirely new attempt to solve the problem: by stopping interference with nature for one day, time is eliminated; where there is no change, no work, no human interference, there is no time. Instead of a Sabbath on which man bows down to the lord of time, the biblical Sabbath symbolizes man's victory over time. Time is suspended; Saturn is dethroned on his very day, Saturn's-day. Death is suspended and life rules on the Sabbath day.*

* It is interesting to speculate whether the basic principle of the Jewish Sabbath might not be practiced on a day of rest (Saturday) different from the day of recreation constituted by our present Sunday, which is devoted to sport, excursions, and so on. Considering the increasing custom of having two free days, such an idea does not seem to be impractical in industrialized countries. When I speak of the principle of the Jewish Sabbath, I am not referring to all the details of the Jewish Sabbath law, such as not carrying even a book or a handkerchief or not lighting a fire. Although I believe that even these details are important to create the full atmosphere of rest, I do not think that—except perhaps for a small minority—one could expect people to follow such cumbersome practices. But I do believe that the principle of the Sabbath rest might be adopted by a much larger number of people—Christians, Jews, and people outside of any religion. The Sabbath day, for them, would be a day of contemplation, reading, meaningful conversation, a day of rest and joy, completely free from all practical and mundane concerns.

vii *The Psalms*

Considering the fact that all the previous chapters of this book have dealt with concepts found throughout the Old Testament and the development of these concepts in the later Jewish tradition, it may seem odd that this last chapter deals with one single book of the Bible, which originated around 400–200 B.C. From a formal point of view this changes the principle of organization I have followed thus far. Yet there are good reasons to include a discussion of the Book of Psalms. The first of these reasons is the special role psalms have played in the religious life of the Jews, especially during the two millennia after the destruction of the Temple.

Psalms (*Sefer Tehillim*), called in the Talmud the "Verses of Praise," were sung in the Temple by a choir of Levites, accompanied by stringed and wind instruments. While not all of them were used in this way, the book as a whole may fairly be described as the "hymnal of the Temple." *

After the destruction of the Temple, Psalms became the most popular prayer book among the Jews. The psalms ceased to be a part of the Temple ritual and assumed a new function: they became a human document, the expression of man's hopes and fears, his joys and his sorrows. They transcended the particular conditions of time and religious dogma and became the intimate friends and companions of Jews and Christians over many generations.

The reason for closing this book with a chapter on the psalms lies, however, not only in their role as just described. I want to call attention to different types of religious experience by analyzing different kinds of *psychic attitudes* that find expression in the Psalter. This is an approach quite different from the one taken by the critical literature dealing with the psalms. Originally this literature was concerned with the problem of authorship and times of origin. The newer critical approach to Psalms is less concerned with authorship than with the particular function they played in the life of Israel, as expressed in their content.† Hermann Gunkel, one of the leading exponents of this critical literature dealing with Psalms, finds the following types, or "classes" (*Gattungen*):

1) Hymns, or songs of praise; a special class is formed by the "enthronement psalms."

* *The Psalms*, edited by A. Cohen (Hindhead, Surrey: The Soncino Press, 1945), p. x.

† Cf. W. O. E. Oesterley, *The Psalms* (London: S.P.C.K., 1953).

2) Laments of the community.
3) Royal psalms.
4) Laments of the individual.
5) Thanksgiving of the individual.

Oesterley adds several smaller classes:

6) Blessings and curses.
7) Pilgrim psalms.
8) Thanksgiving of the Israelite nation.
9) Legends.
10) Psalms dealing with the law.
11) Prophetic psalms.
12) Wisdom psalms.*

There are other similar classifications of the contents of Psalms, and quite obviously it is often debatable which are the most fitting categories under which each psalm is to be classified. But while I appreciate the value of such purely descriptive classification, this chapter tries to introduce another type of classification which has to do primarily with the subjective state of mind, the "mood," in which each psalm is written. The two main classes of psalms, as far as this subjective element is concerned, are:

1) The *one-mood* psalms (of which there are sixty-six).

2) The *dynamic* psalms (of which there are forty-seven).

To these two main categories, two further classifications can be added:

3) The *hymnic* psalms (of which there are thirteen).

4) The *messianic* psalms (of which there are twenty-four).†

* W. O. E. Oesterley, *ibid.*, p. 6.

† The figures given here are approximate ones. Quite a few psalms could be placed in a category other than the one in which they have been classified here. Nevertheless, the classification given shows a rough picture of the number of psalms in each group.

What is the character of the one-mood psalm? It is written in one mood, regardless of what the mood is. We find in this category psalms of hope, of fear, of hate, of peace and contentment, of self-righteousness. What they all have in common is that the poet remains in the same mood from the beginning to the end of the psalm. His words express his mood, they describe it in many facets, but *he* remains the same. He is a hopeful, a frightened, a hating, a self-righteous, or a contented man, and during the recitation of the psalm there is no movement within him, no change of the "key" in which he started.

In the following I shall give some examples of various types of the one-mood psalms; the first one is Psalm 1:

1   Blessed is the man
        who walks not in the counsel of the wicked,
        nor stands in the way of sinners,
        nor sits in the seat of scoffers;
2   but his delight is in the law of the Lord,
        and on his law he meditates day and night.

3   He is like a tree
        planted by streams of water,
      that yields its fruit in its season,
        and its leaf does not wither.
      In all that he does, he prospers.

4   The wicked are not so,
        but are like chaff which the wind drives away.
5   Therefore the wicked will not stand in the judgment,
        nor sinners in the congregation of the righteous;
6   for the Lord knows the way of the righteous,
      but the way of the wicked will perish.

This is a good example of the self-righteous mood. The poet knows he is good, that God will reward him, and that

the wicked will perish. He is not afraid or doubtful; the
world is as it should be, and he is "on the right side."

Psalm 23 is also a one-mood psalm, yet the content of the
mood is markedly different. The elements of smugness,
self-righteousness, and indignation are lacking, and instead
we find a mood of quiet confidence and inner peace:

1 The Lord is my shepherd, I shall not want;
2 he makes me lie down in green pastures.
 He leads me beside still waters;
3 he restores my soul.
 He leads me in paths of righteousness
  for his name's sake.

4 Even though I walk through the valley of the
      shadow of death,
  I fear no evil;
 for thou art with me;
  thy rod and thy staff,
  they comfort me.

5 Thou preparest a table before me
  in the presence of my enemies;
 thou anointest my head with oil,
  my cup overflows.
6 Surely goodness and mercy shall follow me
  all the days of my life;
 and I shall dwell in the house of the Lord for ever.

The same mood is expressed in Psalm 121:

1 I lift up my eyes to the hills.
 From whence does my help come?
2 My help comes from the Lord,
  who made heaven and earth.

3   He will not let your foot be moved,
         he who keeps you will not slumber.
4   Behold, he who keeps Israel
         will neither slumber nor sleep.

5   The Lord is your keeper;
         the Lord is your shade
         on your right hand.
6   The sun shall not smite you by day,
         nor the moon by night.

7   The Lord will keep you from all evil;
         he will keep your life.
8   The Lord will keep
         your going out and your coming in
         from this time forth and for evermore.

These two psalms are among the most beautiful expressions of the mood of hope and faith, and it is no wonder that they have come to be two of the best-known and most loved poems in the Psalter.

Psalm 137 falls into a different type of this category. Here the mood is not one of inner peace or self-righteousness but one of merciless hate:

1   By the waters of Babylon,
         there we sat down and wept,
             when we remembered Zion.
2   On the willows there
         we hung up our lyres.
3   For there our captors
         required of us songs,
     and our tormentors, mirth, saying,
             "Sing us one of the songs of Zion!"

4   How shall we sing the Lord's song
         in a foreign land?

5   If I forget you, O Jerusalem,
        let my right hand wither!
6   Let my tongue cleave to the roof of my mouth,
        if I do not remember you,
     if I do not set Jerusalem
        above my highest joy!

7   Remember, O Lord, against the Edomites
        the day of Jerusalem,
     how they said, "Rase it, rase it!
        Down to its foundations!"
8   O daughter of Babylon, you devastator!
        Happy shall he be who requites you
        with what you have done to us!
9   Happy shall he be who takes your little ones
        and dashes them against the rock!

These few examples may suffice to convey the meaning of
the concept of the one-mood psalm. But I hope this concept
will be still further clarified by the understanding of the
nature of the dynamic psalms.

The essential feature of the dynamic psalm consists in the
fact that a change of mood is going on within the poet,
a change that is reflected in the psalm. What happens is
that the poet begins the psalm in a mood of sadness,
depression, despair, or fear; usually, in fact, it is a blend of
these various moods. At the end of the psalm his mood has
changed; it is one of hope, faith, confidence. Often it seems
as if the poet who composed the end of the psalm was a
different man from the one who composed the beginning.
Indeed, they are different, yet they are the same person.
What happens is that a change has occurred within the
Psalmist during the composition of the psalm. He has been
transformed; or better, he has transformed himself from a
despairing and anxious man into one of hope and faith.

The dynamic psalm shows the inner struggle within the poet to rid himself of despair and to arrive at hope. Thus we find that the movement takes on the following form: it starts in some despair, changes to some hope, then returns to deeper despair and reacts with more hope; eventually it arrives at the very deepest despair and only at this point is the despair really overcome. The mood has definitely changed, and in the following verses of the psalm there is no experience of despair, except as a receding memory. The psalm is the expression of a struggle, a movement, an active process occurring within a person; while in the one-mood psalm the poet wants to confirm an existing feeling, in the dynamic psalm his aim is to transform himself in the process of saying the psalm. The psalm is a document of the victory of hope over despair. It also documents an important fact: that only when the frightened, despairing person experiences the full depth of his despair can he "return," can he liberate himself from despair and achieve hope. As long as the full despair has not been experienced, he cannot really overcome it. He may overcome it for a while, only to fall back into it after a time. The cure of despair is not achieved by encouraging thoughts, not even by feeling *part* of the despair; it is achieved by the seeming paradox that despair *can be overcome only if it has been fully experienced.**

In the following I shall give some examples of dynamic psalms. Psalm 6 is one of the simpler ones that fall into

* This principle, which is so manifest in the dynamic psalms, is actually the same which is followed by the psychoanalytic method. Only by making the painful unconscious conscious (be it despair, fear, hate), which means to become aware of that which one is not aware of, can one liberate oneself from that which has been brought into awareness. This principle holds true in the case of despair as well as in that of other repressed emotions.

this category, and for this reason is particularly useful as an introduction to this type of psalm:

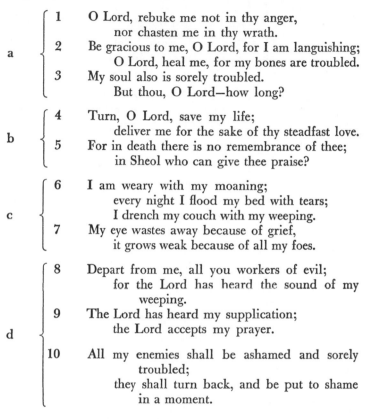

a

1 O Lord, rebuke me not in thy anger,
      nor chasten me in thy wrath.
2 Be gracious to me, O Lord, for I am languishing;
      O Lord, heal me, for my bones are troubled.
3 My soul also is sorely troubled.
      But thou, O Lord—how long?

b

4 Turn, O Lord, save my life;
      deliver me for the sake of thy steadfast love.
5 For in death there is no remembrance of thee;
      in Sheol who can give thee praise?

c

6 I am weary with my moaning;
      every night I flood my bed with tears;
      I drench my couch with my weeping.
7 My eye wastes away because of grief,
      it grows weak because of all my foes.

d

8 Depart from me, all you workers of evil;
      for the Lord has heard the sound of my
      weeping.
9 The Lord has heard my supplication;
      the Lord accepts my prayer.

10 All my enemies shall be ashamed and sorely
      troubled;
      they shall turn back, and be put to shame
      in a moment.

If we analyze the dynamics of this psalm we find the following:

The first stanza (a) expresses fear, but there is an element of hope, a turning to God for help. In the second stanza (b) there is some hope and appeal to God. The third stanza (c) contains the full expression of despair. There is no hope

and no turning to God. The poet has touched the very depth
of his despair and expresses it fully, without trying to soften
it by appealing to God.

At this point the decisive turn occurs. Without any transition the turn is made in the following stanza (d). Suddenly
and unexpectedly the poet seems to have overcome all fear
and despair, and says: "Depart from me, all you workers
of evil; for the Lord *has heard* the sound of my weeping."
The crucial part of this sentence is the perfect tense in "the
Lord *has heard* [*shama*]." There is no more supplication or
prayer; there is certainty. The poet, in one moment, has
jumped from the mood of despair to that of certainty. The
miracle has happened. Not a miracle that comes from the
outside but a miracle that takes place inside man. Despair
can be overcome by hope. The transition is sudden because
there can be nothing but a sudden transition. The transformation from one mood to the other is not a slow change;
it is not a self-persuasion about feeling better and better;
it is a sudden revelationlike experience which has the
premise of having been fully immersed in despair. The psalm
ends with a verse which expresses the conviction that "the
enemies shall turn back and be put to shame in a moment."
This last verse explains that the first part of the psalm
dealt with a despair caused by powerful enemies; logically,
when the despair is overcome, the fear of the enemies also
ceases. But it does not matter particularly whether fear of
enemies is part of the picture; what matters is the change
that takes place within the poet's heart.

Psalm 8 is a dynamic one of a very different nature. While
in Psalm 6 the mood moves from open and intense despair to
hope and confidence, Psalm 8 expresses no such despair or
fear. It is a philosophical psalm, the theme of which is the

powerlessness of man—and yet the experience of his grandeur.

<table>
<tr><td rowspan="3">a</td><td>1</td><td>O Lord, our Lord,
how majestic is thy name in all the earth,
Thou who hast set thy glory above the heavens! *</td></tr>
<tr><td>2</td><td>By the mouth of babes and infants,
thou hast founded a bulwark because of thy foes,
to still the enemy and the avenger.</td></tr>
</table>

	1	O Lord, our Lord,
		  how majestic is thy name in all the earth,
		  Thou who hast set thy glory above the heavens! *

a	2	By the mouth of babes and infants, thou hast founded a bulwark because of thy foes, to still the enemy and the avenger.

	3	When I look at thy heavens, the work of thy
		  fingers,
		  the moon and the stars which thou hast
		  established;

b	4	what is man that thou art mindful of him,
		  and the son of man that thou dost care for
		  him?

	5	Yet thou hast made him little less than God, and dost crown him with glory and honor,

	6	Thou hast given him dominion over the works
		  of thy hands;
		  thou hast put all things under his feet,

c	7	all sheep and oxen, and also the beasts of the field,
	8	the birds of the air, and the fish of the sea, whatever passes along the paths of the sea.
	9	O Lord, our Lord, how majestic is thy name in all the earth!

* I have quoted in the last line of the first verse Oesterley's translation, which is the same as that suggested in Cohen's *The Psalms*. The *Revised Standard Version* translates "whose glory above the heavens is chanted," but in view of the fact that the meaning of the verb is doubtful, both Oesterley and Cohen suggest the reading "who hast set" (*nasata* for *t'nah*). It will become clearer in the text why this translation also makes more sense from the standpoint of the structure of the psalm.

The first stanza (a) begins, "O Lord, our Lord, how majestic is thy name in all the earth, Thou who has set thy glory above the heavens!" The second verse confirms the faith of the author: the babes and infants manifest God's strength. But in stanza (b) the mood of hope and confidence is interrupted. In this stanza there is no open fear or despair, but there is a deep doubt, the experience of man's smallness and weakness as compared with nature and God. And again, suddenly in the second part of the psalm, the mood of doubt is overcome. Stanza (c) expresses enthusiastic confidence in man's strength and power.* To the question, "What is man?" here the answer is: "Yet thou hast made him little less than God" (or, "gods"). Then the stanza continues by portraying man as the master of all nature. The last verse repeats the first, with an important difference, however: the last verse omits "Thou who has set thy glory above the heavens." In the beginning the poet feels that while God's glory is also on the earth, it is nevertheless in heaven. The psalm ends in the full confirmation of *this* life and man's strength on this earth; the second part of the verse disappears from the picture. The thought of heaven is eliminated in order to emphasize fully that this earth, and man on it, is full of God's glory.

In some respects, Psalm 90 is similar to Psalm 8:

a	1	Lord, thou hast been our dwelling place in all generations.
	2	Before the mountains were brought forth, or ever thou hadst formed the earth and the world, from everlasting to everlasting thou art God.

* It is a mood which could have been expressed by Pico della Mirandola and other Renaissance philosophers.

b

  3   Thou turnest man back to the dust,
       and sayest, "Turn back, O children of men!
  4   For a thousand years in thy sight
       are but as yesterday when it is past,
       or as a watch in the night.

  5   Thou dost sweep men away; they are like a
       dream,
       like grass which is renewed in the morning:
  6   in the morning it flourishes and is renewed;
       in the evening it fades and withers.

  7   For we are consumed by thy anger;
       by thy wrath we are overwhelmed.
  8   Thou hast set our iniquities before thee,
       our secret sins in the light of thy countenance.

  9   For all our days pass away under thy wrath,
       our years come to an end like a sigh.
10   The years of our life are threescore and ten,
       or even by reason of strength fourscore;
     yet their span is but toil and trouble;
       they are soon gone, and we fly away.
11   Who considers the power of thy anger,
       and thy wrath according to the fear of thee?
12   So teach us to number our days
       that we may get a heart of wisdom.

c

13   Return, O Lord! How long?
       Have pity on thy servants!
14   Satisfy us in the morning with thy steadfast love,
       that we may rejoice and be glad all our days.
15   Make us glad as many days as thou hast afflicted
       us,
       and as many years as we have seen evil.
16   Let thy work be manifest to thy servants,
       and thy glorious power to their children.
17   Let the favor of the Lord our God be upon us,
       and establish thou the work of our hands
         upon us,
       yea, the work of our hands establish thou it.

Stanza (a) begins in a tone of confidence and hope. But with stanza (b) the mood changes radically. These verses (as in Psalm 8) are not expressions of personal fright and despair, but of a more impersonal, philosophical, depressed mood, rooted in the awareness of the powerlessness of man and the futility of all earthly expectations. With stanza (c) the mood changes. As in some other psalms the change is introduced by addressing God directly: "Return, O Lord! How long?" This line is the expression of great intimacy and confidence. These are the words a lover might speak to the beloved who, in a fit of anger, has turned away, and yet of whose return he is sure. The same verse continues: "Repent * concerning thy servants" and goes on from verses 14 to 17 in a mood of confidence which has an almost hymnic character. Sorrow over the powerlessness of man and the futility of life has given way to a jubilant expression of confidence in man's power, in the work of his hands: "and establish thou the work of our hands upon us, yea, the work of our hands establish thou it."

Perhaps the most beautiful example of the dynamic group is Psalm 22:

a
    1   My God, my God, why hast thou forsaken me?
        Why art thou so far from helping
            me, from the words of my groaning?
    2   O my God, I cry by day, but thou dost not answer;
        and by night, but find no rest.

* The Hebrew text *vehiniahem* can be translated as "have pity" (or, "compassion") or as "repent" (as for instance by Oesterley). To ask God to repent is an expression of greater self-affirmation and confidence than to ask for pity; hence I believe that Oesterley's translation fits better into the mood of this verse.

3 Thou, holy one,*
   enthroned on the praises of Israel.

4 In thee our fathers trusted;

b   they trusted, and thou didst deliver them.

5 To thee they cried, and were saved;
   in thee they trusted, and were not disappointed.

6 But I am a worm, and no man;
   scorned by men, and despised by the people.

7 All who see me mock at me,

c   they make mouths at me, they wag their
   heads;

8 "He committed his cause to the Lord,
   let him deliver him,
 let him rescue him, for he delights in him!"

9 Yet thou art he who took me from the womb;
   thou made me trust in my mother's breasts,†

10 Upon thee was I cast from my birth,
   and since my mother bore me thou hast been

d   my God.

11 Be not far from me,
   for trouble is near
   and there is none to help.

* In most translations this line is rendered "Yet thou art holy." To make a statement about the holiness of God is a modification of the text, which says "And thou, holy one." The Hebrew text, as it is, does not warrant such an alteration. The exclamation "Thou, holy one" is an expression of the poet's turning to God; the "Thou" is a word of love, of intimacy. The translators have not understood the dramatic and dynamic style of this psalm. Here a man is not talking *about* God but talking *to* God in full intimacy.

† The translation in the *Revised Standard Version,* "Thou didst keep me safe upon my mother's breasts," is possible, but unlikely. The text says *mavtihi,* which *can* mean "to make secure"; but it means also, and certainly does in this case, "to cause me to trust." (Cf. Gesenius, *Lexicon.*)

12   Many bulls encompass me,
        strong bulls of Bashan surround me;
13   they open wide their mouths at me,
        like a ravening and roaring lion.

14   I am poured out like water,
        and all my bones are out of joint;
     my heart is like wax,
        it is melted within my breast;
15   my strength is dried up like a potsherd;
        and my tongue cleaves to my jaws;
        thou dost lay me in the dust of death.

e

16   Yea, dogs are round about me;
        a company of evildoers encircle me;
        they have pierced my hands and feet—
17   I can count all my bones—
        they stare and gloat over me;
18   they divide my garments among them,
        and for my raiment they cast lots.

f

19   But thou, O Lord, be not far off!
        O thou my help, hasten to my aid!
20   Deliver my soul from the sword,
        my life from the power of the dog!
21   Save me from the mouth of the lion,
        and from the horns of the wild oxen
     *Thou has answered me.**

g

22   I will tell of thy name to my brethren;
        in the midst of the congregation I will praise
           thee:
23   You who fear the Lord, praise him!
        all you sons of Jacob, glorify him,
        and stand in awe of him, all you sons of
           Israel!

---

* My translation, E.F.; it is crucial for the understanding of the psalm to translate correctly the Hebrew term *anitani*.

h
$\left\{\begin{array}{l}\text{24}\end{array}\right.$ 24 For he has not despised or abhorred
        the affliction of the afflicted;
        and he has not hid his face from him,
        but has heard, when he cried to him.

i
25 From thee comes my praise in the great congre-
        gation;
        my vows I will pay before those who fear
        him.

j
26 The afflicted shall eat and be satisfied;
        those who seek him shall praise the Lord!
        May your hearts live for ever!

k
27 All the ends of the earth shall remember
        and turn to the Lord;
        and all the families of the nations
        shall worship before him.

28 For dominion belongs to the Lord,
        and he rules over the nations.

29 Yea, to him shall all the proud of the earth bow
        down;
        before him shall bow all who go down to
        the dust,
        and he who cannot keep himself alive.

30 Posterity shall serve him;
        men shall tell of the Lord to the coming
        generation,

31 and proclaim his deliverance to a people yet
        unborn,
        that he has wrought it.

Stanza (a) expresses deep despair. The poet cries to God, but God does not hear him. The next stanza (b) expresses hope. It begins with the words "And thou [*ve-atah*] holy one [*kadosh*]," and then it seeks consolation in the memory that God helped the poet's fathers: "in thee they trusted, and were not disappointed."

But remembering God's help to his fathers is not enough
to make the poet move out of his despair. He falls back into
it, and even more intensely. This new move into despair is
expressed in stanza (c). Again despair is followed by new
hope and faith in stanza (d), a faith which seems deeper than
that expressed in stanza (b); this time the poet does not recall
the fathers but the mother. The text says: "For Thou took
me out of the womb and made me trust in my mother's
breasts." This phrase is a beautiful expression of the original
trust, the "original faith," with which the child is endowed.
It is the faith in the mother's unconditional love; the faith
that she will nurse him when he is hungry, cover him when
he is cold, comfort him when he is in pain. The mother's
love is experienced at an earlier age than the father's; it is
expressed in the unmistakable language of the body, and is
not dependent on any condition. Hence, to remember the
mother's love is the most reassuring memory for one who
feels lost and abandoned.

But not even this memory helps the poet to emerge from
his despair. With renewed vigor he is assailed by fright
and loneliness, and this third attack of despair is expressed
in stanza (e), which is twice as long as the previous ones. A
new stanza starts with verse 19. It begins with the word
"Thou," and again the poet turns toward God. He is no
longer lost, as in the previous stanza, in the expression of
despair, but he turns to God and asks for salvation. He says:

> "Thou! Lord! do not be far,
> My strength, hasten to help me.
> Save my soul from the sword,
> My only one [my life] from the power of the dog.
> Save me from the lion's mouth
> And from the horns of the wild oxen.
> Thou hast answered me."

While the first verses of this stanza are still worded in the form of a prayer, the last line, "Thou hast answered me," changes the form of the prayer; suddenly there is certainty that the Lord *has* saved him. There is no logical or psychological transition here; the change of mood occurs like a flash of lightning, with hardly any preparation. The poet has touched and expressed the depth of his despair—and like a miracle something happens in him so that he has faith and hope. If one does not understand the nature of this inner movement one is almost forced to consider the text either corrupt or not worth paying any attention to. Thus the *Revised Standard Version* translates this verse as "Save me from the mouth of the lion, my afflicted soul from the horn of the wild oxen." In this way "Thou hast answered me" is simply eliminated, in order to avoid the difficulty of the sudden use of the perfect tense.*

That this last phrase ("Thou has answered me") is by no means corrupt or meaningless is shown in the next stanza (g). Instead of the mood of despair and sorrow, a mood of hope and enthusiasm fills the heart of the poet. Unless one wants to assume that this is a different psalm—and most critics do not assume this—then it is clear that the decisive turn has occurred within one moment, when the poet was able to say: *Thou hast answered me.* He is a new man since he has spoken this word, a man who can now sing a hymn of praise and enthusiasm. His despair has now been transformed into the memory of something that once happened (stanza

---

* The translation of The Jewish Publication Society of America says "answer me" instead of "thou *hast* answered me." Oesterley translates in the same way as the *Revised Standard Version*, remarking: "The Hebrew text reads, 'Thou hast answered me from the horns of the wild oxen,' which is meaningless."

h), followed by new praise (i), and again followed by the memory of past suffering (j). The last stanza (k) consists of five verses and no longer contains even the memory of despair. It expresses unmitigated hope, faith, and enthusiasm, and ends with another "perfect"—the certainty *ki-asah*, "he has wrought it." The last verses are said in a mood of enthusiasm and of messianic hope for the deliverance of all mankind.

The movement from sadness to joy is in part also visible in the Psalter as a whole. While it does not start with despair in the first psalm, it ends with psalms which express a mood of unmitigated joy.

The movement of the dynamic psalms has continued in the later Jewish tradition and found its most distinct and beautiful expression two thousand years later in the songs of Hasidism. Many of these songs, which were usually sung by the Hasidic master together with his adherents on Saturday afternoons, have exactly the same inner movement as the dynamic psalms of the Bible. They begin in a mood of sadness and end in enthusiastic joy; this movement is, in fact, often repeated in the following way: * first, the song itself has a movement which leads from sadness to joy. Secondly, the song is repeated many times, and each repetition is more joyful than the previous one; at the end, the *whole* song has become a hymn of joy. A good example is the famous "Rav's Nigun," the song created by R. Schneur Zalman, the founder

---

* There is a great wealth of Hasidic songs; they have mostly been transmitted orally. (I learned many from my teacher, S. B. Rabinkow.) A good collection of songs that have been written down is to be found in Chemjo Vinaver, *An Anthology of Jewish Music* (New York: Edward B. Marks, 1955).

of the Habad branch of Hasidism. It consists of three movements, beginning with sadness and ending in joy.*

The other two categories of psalms I have mentioned, the
messianic and the hymnic psalms, are really also one-mood.
I have classified them separately because the mood in which
they are written has a different quality from that of the
other one-mood psalms. It is not the mood of contentment,
righteousness, or despair, but in the messianic psalms the
mood is one of faith in the salvation of mankind,† and in
the hymnic psalms, the mood is one of pure enthusiasm.

One example of a messianic psalm is Psalm 96:

1   O sing to the Lord a new song;
        sing to the Lord, all the earth!
2   Sing to the Lord, bless his name;
        tell of his salvation from day to day.
3   Declare his glory among the nations,
        his marvelous works among all the peoples!
4   For great is the Lord, and greatly to be praised;
        he is to be feared above all gods.
5   For all the gods of the peoples are idols;
        but the Lord made the heavens.
6   Honor and majesty are before him;
        strength and beauty are in his sanctuary.

* The same dynamics can also be found in the chanting of the
classical Kol Nidrei on the eve of the Day of Atonement. The
melody is repeated three times, in an increasingly loud voice each
time. I have little doubt that what is meant by "louder voice" is a
more enthusiastic mood, instead of the subdued mood in which
it is begun.

† Sometimes this faith is expressed only in the last verses of the
psalm (for instance, in Psalm 53), and one might doubt whether
this justifies classifying this and other psalms with the messianic
ones, as far as the mood of the entire psalm is concerned.

7   Ascribe to the Lord, O families of the peoples,
      ascribe to the Lord glory and strength!
8   Ascribe to the Lord the glory due his name;
      bring an offering, and come into his courts!
9   Worship the Lord in holy array;
      tremble before him, all the earth!
10 Say among the nations, "The Lord reigns!
      Yea, the world is established, it shall never be
        moved;
      he will judge the peoples with equity."
11 Let the heavens be glad, and let the earth rejoice;
      let the sea roar, and all that fills it;
12   let the field exult, and everything in it!
      Then shall all the trees of the wood sing for joy
13   before the Lord, for he comes,
      for he comes to judge the earth.
    He will judge the world with righteousness,
      and the peoples with his truth.

It will suffice here if I quote an outstanding example of the
category of the hymnic psalms, the last in the Psalter, Psalm
150:

a
    1   Praise the Lord!
        Praise God in his sanctuary;
          praise him in his mighty firmament!
    2   Praise him for his mighty deeds;
          praise him according to his exceeding
            greatness!

b
    3   Praise him with trumpet sound;
          praise him with lute and harp!
    4   Praise him with timbrel and dance;
          praise him with strings and pipe!
    5   Praise him with sounding cymbals:
          praise him with loud clashing cymbals!
    6   Let everything that breathes praise the Lord!
        Praise the Lord!

In this psalm there is little content; in the first stanza (vv. 1–2) God's deeds are praised; in the second (3–6) there is nothing but the rhythm of joy, expressed in terms of all the instruments that praise God. But above the instrument is life itself. And, hence, this Ode to Joy ends with the words: "Let everything that breathes praise the Lord! Praise the Lord!"

viii *Epilogue*

I have tried to show the development of the concept of God and man within the Old Testament and the post-biblical Jewish tradition. We have seen that it begins with an authoritarian God and an obedient man, but even in this authoritarian structure the seeds of freedom and independence are already to be found. From the very beginning God is to be obeyed precisely in order to prevent men from obeying idols. The worship of the one God is the negation of the worship of men and things.

The development of biblical and post-biblical ideas represents the growth of this seed. God, the authoritarian ruler, becomes God the constitutional monarch, who is himself

bound by the principles he has announced. The anthropo-
morphically described God becomes a nameless God, and
eventually a God of whom no essential attribute can be predicated. Man, the obedient servant, becomes the free man,
who makes his own history, free from God's interference and
guided only by the prophetic message, which he can either
accept or reject.*

As I have pointed out, however, there were limits to which
man's freedom from God could be conceptualized: the same
limits exist with regard to the possibility of discarding the
very concept of God. They are natural to a religion which
wishes to provide formulations of a unifying principle and
symbol by which to "cement" its structure and hold its believers together. Hence, the Jewish religion could not take
the last logical step, to give up "God" and to establish a concept of man as a being who is alone in this world, but who
can feel at home in it if he achieves union with his fellow
man and with nature.

I have tried to show that the God-concept is only "the finger
that points to the moon." This moon is not outside of ourselves but is the human reality behind the words: what we
call the *religious attitude* is an x that is expressible only in
poetic and visual symbols. This x experience has been articu-
lated in various concepts which have varied in accordance
with the social organization of a particular cultural period.

* Why older conceptualizations are carried along, even though the
substance behind the thought has changed, is beautifully expressed
by Max Müller in his *Vedanta Philosophy* (London: Sugil Gupta
[India Ltd.], 1894): "We all know from our own experience that
what has been handed down to us as very ancient, and what as
children we have been taught to consider as sacred, retains through
life a fascination which is difficult to shake off altogether. Every
attempt to discover reason in what is unreasonable is considered as
legitimate so long as it enables us to keep what we are unwilling to
part with" (page 62).

In the Near East, x was expressed in the concept of a supreme tribal chief, or king, and thus "God" became the supreme concept of Judaism, Christianity, and Islam, which were rooted in the social structures of that area. In India, Buddhism could express x in different forms, so that no concept of God as a supreme ruler was necessary.

However, inasmuch as both believers and unbelievers strive for the same aim—the liberation and awakening of man—they both can appreciate, each in his own way, that love impels us to understand the other better than he understands himself. Thus, those who believe in God will think that the nonbelieving humanist is in error, as far as his thought concepts are concerned, and vice versa. But both will know that they are united in their common goal, which can be discovered more from their actions than from their concepts. Above all, they will be united by their common fight against idolatry.

The Idolators, too, are to be found among both believers and nonbelievers. Such believers have made God into an idol, an omniscient, omnipotent power allied with those who have power on this earth. Similarly, there are unbelievers who do not accept God, but worship other idols (which are also those of many believers) : the sovereign state, the flag, the race, material production and efficiency, political leaders, or themselves.

Those, however, who worship God in an unalienated fashion, and those who strive for the same goal in purely human terms, recognize that thought concepts are secondary to the human reality behind the thought. They both understand the meaning of a Hasidic story about an adherent of a Hasidic master who was asked whether he visited his master to hear his words of wisdom. "No," he answered, "I want to see how he ties his shoelaces."

Anyone, believer or not, who has experienced the value
x as the supreme value and tries to realize it in his life, cannot help recognizing that most men in industrial society, in
spite of their protestations, are not striving for this value.
These are anxious, vacuous, and isolated consumers, bored
with life and compensating for their chronic depression
by compulsive consumption. Ever more attracted to things
and gadgets than to life and growth, they are men whose aim
is to *have* much and to *use* much, not to *be* much.

This whole book touches upon a question which has been
given increasing attention in the last few years: Is God dead?
The question should be divided in its two aspects: Is the
concept of God dead or is the *experience* to which the concept points, and the supreme *value* which it expresses, dead?

In the first case one might formulate the question by asking: Is Aristotle dead? This is because it is largely due to the
Aristotelian influence that God as a thought-concept became
so important and "theology" arose. As far as the God-concept
is concerned, we must also ask whether we should continue
to use a concept which can be understood only in terms of
its social-cultural roots: the Near Eastern cultures, with their
authoritarian tribal chiefs and omnipotent kings; and later
medieval feudalism and absolute monarchies. For the contemporary world, which is no longer guided by Aristotle's
systematic thought and by the idea of kingship, the God-
concept has lost its philosophical and its social basis.*

On the other hand, if what we mean to ask is whether the

---

* The atheistic position prevalent in the nineteenth century suffers
from the same bias as the theistic position, that of making the *concept* of God the main issue rather than the values which it symbolizes.
Atheism was essentially a declaration of independence from the principle of the supreme ruler rather than an answer to the spiritual
problem of man.

experience is dead, then instead of asking whether God is dead, we might better raise the question whether *man is dead.* This seems to be the central problem of man in twentieth-century industrial society. He is in danger of becoming a thing, of being more and more alienated, of losing sight of the real problems of human existence and of no longer being interested in the answers to these problems. If man continues in this direction, he will himself be dead, and the problem of God, as a concept or as a poetic symbol of the highest value, will not be a problem any more.

The central issue today is to recognize this danger and to strive for conditions which will help to bring man to life again. These conditions lie in the realm of fundamental changes in the socioeconomic structure of industrialized society (both of capitalist and socialist societies) and of a renaissance of humanism that focuses on the reality of experienced values rather than on the reality of concepts and words. In the West, this renaissance of humanism is occurring today among adherents of Catholicism, Protestantism, and Judaism, as well as Marxist Socialism. It is a reaction to the two-toed threat which mankind faces today: that of nuclear extinction and that of the transformation of men into appendices of machines. If the spirit and the hopes of the Prophets are to prevail, it will depend on the strength and vitality of this new humanism. For the nontheistic humanists a further question arises: What could take the place of religion in a world in which the concept of God may be dead but in which the experiential reality behind it must live?

ix *Appendix:*
PSALM 22 AND
THE PASSION

Psalm 22 has played a decisive role in the story of the crucifixion of Jesus. Matthew 27:46 reports: "And about the
ninth hour Jesus cried with a loud voice: 'Eli, Eli lama
sabachthani?' that is, 'My God, my God, why hast thou forsaken me?' " (The Gospel quotes the Aramaic version of the
Hebrew text, which reads *Eli, Eli lamaha azavtani.*)

It is an almost unbelievable idea that Jesus should have
died with words of utter despair. This has, of course, been
noted by many interpreters of the Gospel, who explain the
apparent absurdity by pointing to the fact that Jesus was
God *and* man, and as man he died in despair. This explanation is not very satisfactory. There have been many human

martyrs, before and after Jesus, who died in full faith and showing no trace of despair. Thus, for instance, the Talmud reports that R. Akiba, while being tortured, smiled, and when asked by the Roman general why he smiled, answered: "All my life I have prayed: You shall love the Lord, your God, with all your heart, with all your soul [meaning life] and with all your power. I never could love him 'with all my life' until now. That is why I am happy." * Why, then, should Jesus have died in despair as an expression of his being human?

The answer to this puzzling question seems to be simple. In the Jewish tradition up to this day, the books of the Pentateuch, or weekly portions of it, or some prayers, are cited by the first major word or sentence. Some psalms are also still cited by the first words or sentence. For instance *Ashrei* (Psalm 1), or *Al naharot Bavel* (Psalm 137). It is likely that at the time of the first Gospels, Psalm 22, in analogy to this usage, was also cited by its first major sentence. In other words, the Gospel tells us that Jesus, when he was dying, recited Psalm 22. This being so, there is no problem to be solved. As we have seen, the psalm begins in despair, but it ends in an enthusiastic mood of faith and hope. In fact, there is hardly any psalm which would be better suited to the enthusiastic and universalistic mood of the early Christians than the end of this psalm: "Posterity shall serve him; men shall tell of the Lord to the coming generation; men proclaim his deliverance to a people yet unborn, that he has wrought it" (In Hebrew *ki-asah* = "that he has done it").

The text of the crucifixion story shows also quite clearly that the writer of the two earliest books of the Gospel (Mat-

* See Jerusalem Talmud, Berakhot IX, 7, 14b; also Babylonian, Berakhot 61b.

thew and Mark) must have had in mind the entire psalm. Thus, Matthew (27:29) speaks of the Roman soldiers who "mocked him." Psalm 22:7 says: "All who see me mock me." Matthew says (27:43): "Let God deliver him now, if he desires him." Psalm 22:8 says: "Let him rescue him, for he delights in him." Matthew 27:35 says: "They divided his garments among them by casting lots." Psalm 22:18 says: "They divide my garments among them, and for my raiment they cast lots." Furthermore, the psalm says: "They have pierced my hands and my feet."

How can we explain that most Christian theologians accepted the idea that Jesus died with words of despair instead of recognizing that he died reciting the Twenty-Second Psalm? The reason seems to lie simply in the fact that Christian scholars did not think of this small and rather unimportant Jewish custom of citing a book or chapter by its first sentence.

Nevertheless it is quite apparent that at some time after the composition of the Matthew and Mark Gospels (the latter reports the same last words said by Jesus), it was felt that these last words spoken by Jesus could lead precisely to the misunderstanding that Jesus had died with words of despair. This is at least made highly probable by the fact that the text of the crucifixion story was changed.*

Indeed, St. Luke reports that Jesus said: "Father, into thy

* This assumption is supported by a statement by A. E. J. Rawlinson, *The Gospel According to St. Mark* (London: Methuen & Co., 1925; reprinted 1960), p. 236, who writes: "It is possible because it was capable of being so interpreted [as an expression of despair] that it was omitted by Luke and softened in texts current in Italy, Gaul and Carthage (Deik) by the substitution of 'Why didst thou reproach me?' (i.e., why didst thou give me over to reproach?) for 'Why didst thou forsake me?' "

hands I commit my spirit." Quite clearly, the intent of this
passage is to show that Jesus died in a spirit opposite to the
one expressed in the first verse of Psalm 22.

In the Gospel According to St. John, the report is still
different. "When Jesus had received the vinegar, he said, 'It
is finished'; and he bowed his head and gave up his spirit"
(19:30). The assumption does not seem too farfetched that
St. John, in order to avoid the misunderstanding that Jesus
died in despair, chose the *last* words of the psalm as a substitute for the first verse. The Greek Gospel has τετέλεσται,
meaning "it has been accomplished." (The Vulgate translates
consummatum est, which has the same meaning.) The question arises here why St. John did not choose the words by
which the Septuagint translates the *ki-asah* of the psalm:
ἐποίησεν, which is the literal translation of *asah,* "he has
done it." The answer to this question may lie in the fact that
the translation *tetelestai* is used for *asah* in Isaiah 55:11,
which means that St. John had a precedent for this translation.* Furthermore, he may have felt that "it has been
accomplished" made more sense than an isolated *epoiesen*
("he has done it"), which makes little sense without quoting
the whole last verse.

While most Christian theologians have accepted the
idea of Jesus' despair and have explained it in different
ways, there are very few who interpret the "Eli, Eli" in the
direction indicated here. As far as I have been able to find
out from learned theologians, only C. H. Dodd in his
According to the Scriptures (1952) clearly indicates that
the first verse introduces the whole psalm. But there are
several authors who in some way or another have tried to
connect the words of Jesus with Psalm 22 as a whole. The

* I owe this suggestion to Father Jean Lefèvbre.

first one to do this was Justin Martyr in the second century. "In his dialogue with Trypho (chap. 98–106) he quotes, as he says, 'the whole psalm' (but actually only through verse 23)." But it is clear to Justin that Jesus spoke only the first verse and that the rest is introduced as a prophecy which is shown to apply to Christ, since he has identified himself with the "I" of the psalm.*

A connection between the verse "Eli, Eli" and the whole psalm has also been made by some later scholars, such as Loisy: "So Ps. XXII dominates all the accounts of the Passion. Nothing more natural than to place its opening words in the mouth of the dying Christ." Similarly B. Weiss: "The Evangelist did not concern himself with the deeper meaning of the words. He simply regarded them as the fulfillment of a prophecy derived from a Messianic psalm." † Rawlinson comments: "It has, of course, often been argued that our Lord during the agony of the Passion may have stayed His soul by the repetition of passages from the Psalter, and that Psalm 22 may have been running in His thoughts. The psalm as a whole is not one of despair; it is the psalm of a righteous sufferer who yet is confident of the love and the protection of the God of all holiness, even unto death." Yet Rawlinson comes to the conclusion that "it may be doubted whether B. Weiss is not right that such an interpretation introduces 'an artificial element of reflection' into 'a moment of immediate feeling'; and on the assumption that our Lord really uttered the words it is better to say

---

* I owe this suggestion to a personal communication from Prof. Krister Stendhal, directed to Prof. James Luther Adams, who asked him about this in response to a request from me. I quote in the text Prof. Stendhal's remarks with reference to Justin.

† Both quotations, Loisy and Weiss, are from A. E. J. Rawlinson, *op. cit.*, p. 236.

frankly that we do not know exactly what was in His mind at the time, that we are here face to face with the supreme mystery of the Saviour's Passion." *

To sum up: considering (a) the difficulty of the idea that the story of the crucifixion should give a picture of a despairing Christ; (b) the fact that the whole of Psalm 22 was in the mind of the writer of the first Gospel as the premise for the story of the Passion; (c) that the later Gospels substituted words of confidence for the words of despair; (d) that St. John most likely used the end of the psalm instead of the beginning; and finally, the Jewish custom of often quoting a book, prayer, or psalm by its first word or sentence, it seems much more reasonable to assume that in Matthew's and Mark's report Jesus recited Psalm 22 than to indulge in speculations attempting to show either why Jesus was in despair or to assume that these words are an unexplainable mystery. Indeed, it seems likely that the authors of the first Gospels were aware of and shared in the particular kind of religious experience that is expressed in the dynamic psalms.

* Rawlinson, *op. cit.*, p. 236.

INDEX

Aaron, 96–98, 102, 103, 104, 107, 110–11
Abrabanel, Isaac ben Judah, 146
Abraham, 19, 22, 26–28, 46, 51, 71, 83, 89–90, 93, 112, 187
Abraham Abulafia of Tudela, 145
Adam, 28, 37, 64, 70, 83, 84, 87, 115, 159, 161; see also Paradise
Akiba, Rabbi, 69, 78, 148, 153, 182, 232
Altizer, Thomas, 57
Amoraim, 136–38
Amos, 14, 38, 65, 118, 124, 125, 129, 169
apocalypse, 133–36, 139–40
Apocrypha, see Bible, Apocrypha
Aristotle, 5, 228
Atonement, Day of, 168, 173, 175–76, 221
Augustine, St., 122
authority, obedience to, 72–75; see also God, obedience to

Bar Kokhba, 139, 143, 146, 148
Babel, Tower of, 24
Baruch, Apocalypse of, 135
Bible
  anthropomorphism in, 8–9, 29
  Apocrypha, 3, 136–37
  contradictions in, 7–8, 10–12
  Hebrew, 1–10, 12, 14, 42, 72
  New Testament, 4, 9
  Old Testament, 3, 4, 5–10, 12, 13, 20, 22, 38, 41, 72, 114, 178, 195, 225
  prophetic writings of, 70, 83
  Psalms, 201–23, 231–36
Bonhoeffer, Dietrich, 57
Buddhism, 61, 118, 227; see also Zen Buddhism

Cain, 161
Calvin, John, 47, 122
Cardozo, Michael, 147
Catholicism, Roman, 4, 122; see also Christianity
Christ, see Jesus of Nazareth
Christianity, 4, 41, 57, 81, 115, 134, 138, 143, 148, 154, 156, 227; see also Catholicism, Roman;

Jesus of Nazareth; Paul of Tarsus, St.; theology, Christian
Cohen, Hermann, 5, 13, 50, 52, 66–67, 182, 183
Communism, 156; see also Marx, Karl
conceptualization, 17–19, 226; see also God, concept of
conscience, 55–56, 58, 87
covenants, the, 24–26, 83, 112, 113, 225–26

Daniel, 124, 125, 133–34
David, 91, 124, 133, 161
Diderot, Denis, 154–55

Eckhart, Master, 19, 31, 62, 176
Elijah, 150
Engels, Friedrich, 156
Enlightenment, the, 14, 122
Enoch, Books of, 135
ethics, see law, moral
Esau, 161
Eve, 28, 64, 70, 83, 116, 159; see also Adam; Paradise
evil, biblical view of, 159–64, 180–81; see also sin
Ezekiel, 124, 125, 170
Ezra, Fourth Book of, 135–36

faith, 157, 206, 207, 218–19, 221, 232
fixation, emotional, 72–73, 90
Frank, Jacob, 147
Freud, Sigmund, 55, 61, 91

Gemara, 5, 9, 10
Gentiles, 51, 56
Geonim, 136
God
  actions of, 37–38, 40, 52–53, 67, 92, 96; see also history, God revealed in
  as absolute ruler, 22–25, 46–47, 64, 77, 225
  as Creator, 6, 63–64
  as judge, 28; see also justice, principle of
  as redeemer, 124; see also man, redemption of
  attributes of, 33–37, 40, 62, 65

237

God (*Continued*)
  concept of, 18–22, 37, 41–42, 49,
    52, 53, 61–62, 225–29
  "death of," 228–29
  evolution of idea of, 22–32, 37
  existence of, 9, 37–38, 40, 42, 52
  holiness of, 65
  imitation by man of, 65–67, 179,
    185, 187–88, 191; see also ha-
    lakhah
  kingdom of, 138; see also mes-
    sianism
  love for man of, 171–73, 185–86;
    see also love, principle of
  man's knowledge of, 33–38, 40,
    50, 52, 67, 115, 121, 179
  name of, 9, 29–32, 47, 50, 95, 96;
    see also idolatry
  obedience to, 73–74, 77, 79
  reverence for life of, 25, 95, 180–
    81
  unreality of, 18–19
  will of, 101
  worship of, 43, 46–52, 61
  see also nature, God revealed in
Goethe, Johann Wolfgang von, 14
grace, 115–16, 123
Guide for the Perplexed, The (Mai-
    monides), 33–35

Habakkuk, 124, 125
Haggai, 124, 125
halakhah, 54, 77–78; see also God,
    imitation of
Haninah ben Hakhinai, 68
Hasidism, 10, 41, 48, 79–81, 96, 145,
    148–52, 174–75, 180, 220, 221
Hebrews, 6, 10, 26, 83, 89
  liberation from Egypt of, 29, 71–
    72, 90–114, 183–84, 187
Hegel, Georg Wilhelm Friedrich, 44
Hellenism, 10
Herder, Johann Gottfried von, 14
Hillel, 11, 182
history
  God revealed in, 29, 31, 53, 93–94,
    96, 117, 118, 121
  power in, 129–30
  see also man, as maker of history
Holy Land, 5; see also Hebrews
hope, 153–57, 206–20, 232
Hosea, 124, 125, 128, 130, 169, 186
humanism
  Jewish, 13–14, 65, 85, 175

radical, 12–15, 227, 229
Renaissance, 14, 95, 122

ibn Ezra, Abraham, 27, 101
ideology, 19–22
idolatry, 7, 9, 29–32, 42–52, 56, 61–
    62, 95, 108, 111–14, 115–16,
    163, 227
Isaac, 89–90
Isaiah, 19, 22, 42, 44–46, 124, 125,
    126–28, 129, 130–31, 186
Islam, 4, 227
Israel, people of, see Hebrews

Jacob, 161
Jaspers, Karl, 21
Jeremiah, 124, 125, 131–32, 169
Jesus of Nazareth, 69, 122, 144, 154,
    156, 231–36
Jews, persecution of, 82, 85, 143,
    147–48, 153
Joel, 124
Jonah, 119
Joseph, 161
Josephus, Flavius, 74–75
Joshua, 114
Judaism, 4, 11, 120
  eighteenth-century, 6
  medieval, 6, 32–33, 36; see also
    ibn Ezra, Abraham; Maimon-
    ides; Nahmonides; Saadia ben
    Joseph; Samuel ben Meir
  modern, 4
  mysticism in, see mysticism, Jewish
  oral tradition of, see Mishnah;
    Talmud
  rabbinical, 137–43, 153, 171–72,
    192; see also Akiba, Rabbi
  secular kingdoms of, 14–15, 115,
    120–21, 124–25; see also nation-
    alism, Jewish
  use of Bible in, 4–6; see also Bible,
    Hebrew
  see also Hebrews; humanism, Jew-
    ish; Jews, persecution of; mon-
    otheism, Jewish; mysticism,
    Jewish; theology, Jewish; uni-
    versalism, Jewish
Judgment, Day of, 125, 135–36; see
    also apocalypse
justice, principle of, 4, 15, 28, 53–54,
    62, 65–66, 67, 114, 133, 172,
    185
Justin Martyr, 235